Perfectly timed, this book enables the contributors and the readers to reflect on both the journey and current state of education for children with SEND. Informative, challenging, heart-warming and heart-breaking, this is a diverse anthology for parents and educators alike. I particularly enjoyed the nuanced personal tales, the essential rage, and complete commitment to a vision where all children have their needs met unconditionally. The interview with Baroness Warnock herself provides a reflective insight to one of *the* seminal pieces of educational parliamentary work of our time.

—*Keziah Featherstone, Head of School,*
Q3 Academy Tipton, UK

This book identifies significant challenges that must be overcome to ensure every child with SEND is served well by the English education system. It puts forward a pragmatic and clear case outlining how the situation might be improved, exploring areas including accountability and inclusion, teacher training and supply, the availability of school places, and attitudes toward children with SEND. This book is essential reading for professionals, parents and policymakers interested in practical ideas to improve the educational experience for children with SEND.

—*Anne Heavey, National Director,*
Whole School SEND, UK

This is a powerful and important publication in which Rob Webster has brought together a diverse range of some of the most important voices in education today. This book provides us with a chastening reminder of the days when the state wrote children off as 'mentally defective' and sent them to schools for the 'educationally sub-normal'. We have come a long way since those dark days, but the real power of this book is that it makes it clear how far we still have to go.

—*Jarlath O'Brien, Director for Schools,*
The Eden Academy, UK

This book is a call to arms and deserves attention. It builds on the educational and moral rationale, and picks up on the strong economic case for inclusion too. Rob Webster has brought a new lens to the inclusion debate, helping us all to think forward, rather than backwards.

—*Margaret Mulholland, Director of Development and*
Research, Swiss Cottage School, Development and
Research Centre, UK

This book is ideal for those working in initial teacher education, whether student teachers, tutors or mentors. It will help readers gain great insights into the past, present and potential future of the complex policy environment for SEND, and the very real practical implications arising from this for pupils, teachers and parents. Importantly, it also offers practical advice and sensible ways forward.

—*Professor Samantha Twiselton OBE, Director of Sheffield Institute of Education, Sheffield Hallam University, UK*

This excellent collection of contributions helps us all to reflect on how far we have travelled since 1978. And it challenges us all for the future. Even if we had fixed the technical, procedural, organisational, professional, curriculum, assessment and funding issues that we have wrestled with over the last 40 years, we would still face the big questions raised here about children's rights, the values of our education system, and the very nature of teaching. This is a great read, full of commitment, dilemmas and contradictions, and essential for anyone contributing to the development of special education in the next 40 years.

—*Philippa Stobbs, Assistant Director, Education and Equalities, Council for Disabled Children, UK*

Including Children and Young People with Special Educational Needs and Disabilities in Learning and Life

Marking the 40th anniversary of the Warnock Enquiry (1978) into special education in the UK and capturing the coverage of a public debate on special educational needs and disabilities (SEND) hosted by the University College London Institute of Education (2018), this volume explores the legacy of the Enquiry, considering how it has impacted on policy and practice relating to SEND and inclusion, and how it will continue to do so.

Offering historical perspectives and drawing on professional and personal experiences, high-profile contributors, including practitioners, researchers, campaigners and parents, reflect on the approaches taken during the Warnock Enquiry and consider how successfully recommendations have been implemented. Reviewing conceptional and practical territory covered by the Warnock Committee, and assessing the current state of the inclusion and education of young people with SEND in the UK, the text sets out broad, evidence-based principles for rethinking inclusive practice and explores topics including:

- the purposes, contribution and impacts of the Warnock Enquiry
- rights-based approaches to the education of children with SEND
- past and present dialogue between mainstream and specialist settings
- challenges faced by parents of children with SEND
- implications of the Enquiry for initial teacher training
- perceptions of SEND in the media
- the relevance of the Enquiry to policy and practice in the years ahead.

This invaluable text will widen current debates by exploring how persistent problems relating to inclusion and the education of children and young people with SEND might be resolved. It is an essential read for researchers, educationalists, practitioners and families involved in the education of children with SEND.

Rob Webster is Associate Professor at the Centre for Inclusive Education, UCL Institute of Education, UK.

Including Children and Young People with Special Educational Needs and Disabilities in Learning and Life

How Far Have We Come Since
the Warnock Enquiry – and
Where Do We Go Next?

**Edited by
Rob Webster**

LONDON AND NEW YORK

Helping Everyone Achieve ▪ ▪ ▪

Centre for
Inclusive Education

First published 2019
by Routledge
2 Park Square, Milton Park, Abingdon, Oxon OX14 4RN

and by Routledge
52 Vanderbilt Avenue, New York, NY 10017

Routledge is an imprint of the Taylor & Francis Group, an informa business

British Library Cataloguing-in-Publication Data
A catalogue record for this book is available from the British Library

Library of Congress Cataloging-in-Publication Data
Names: Webster, Rob, 1976– editor.
Title: Including children and young people with special
educational needs and disabilities in learning and life: how
far have we come since the Warnock enquiry – and where do
we go next? / edited by Rob Webster.
Description: Abingdon, Oxon; New York, NY: Routledge, [2019] |
Includes bibliographical references.
Identifiers: LCCN 2018053018 (print) | LCCN 2018059930 (ebook) |
ISBN 9780429436499 (ebk) | ISBN 9781138348868 (hbk: alk. paper)
Subjects: LCSH: Special education—Great Britain. |
Inclusive education—Great Britain.
Classification: LCC LC3986.G7 (ebook) | LCC LC3986.G7 I52
2019 (print) | DDC 371.9—dc23
LC record available at https://lccn.loc.gov/2018053018

ISBN: 978-1-138-34886-8 (hbk)
ISBN: 978-0-429-43649-9 (ebk)

Typeset in Times New Roman
by codeMantra

MIX
Paper from
responsible sources
FSC™ C013985

Printed in the United Kingdom
by Henry Ling Limited

Contents

Acknowledgements

The credit for the idea for this book goes to Alison Foyle, who, as senior publisher, has now guided me through my fifth book for Routledge Education. My thanks to my UCL IOE colleagues, Emma Wisby and Kate Thomas, for organising the '*What if?*' debate and to the Director of the IOE, Professor Becky Francis, for chairing what was a lively and stimulating discussion. Emma also arranged the interview with Baroness Warnock, which was filmed and edited by John Cobb. My thanks also to Jon Severs, Commissioning Editor at *Tes*, who saw virtue in the idea of covering the 40th anniversary of the Warnock Report in a special edition (published on 4 May 2018) and for curating an excellent and extensive set of contributions.

I must, of course, thank the contributors to this book – especially as the timetable for production meant they spent part of their summer holidays writing! An extended thank you to those who were also panellists on the IOE debate: Tara Flood, Vijita Patel, Klaus Wedell and Sally Phillips. Finally, a big thank you to Baroness Warnock for taking the time to talk to me and for sharing her recollections, reflections and insights on her pioneering work.

Rob Webster
October 2018

Foreword

Dr Adam Boddison

In January 2016, I joined the National Association for Special Educational Needs (nasen) as Chief Executive, and even as a relative newcomer to the world of special educational needs and disabilities (SEND), I was already well aware of the significance of the Warnock Enquiry on modern-day policy and practice. Since then, it has been a privilege to have met so many people, including many of the contributors to this book, who are passionate about ensuring that the needs of children and young people with SEND are properly identified and met.

It is fair to say that I had heard a lot about the book's editor, Rob Webster, well before I met him. It seemed that every school I visited was talking about Rob's work, and he was somewhat of an educational celebrity across both social and educational media. Eventually, it was through our mutual engagement with Whole School SEND[1] that I first met Rob, and he absolutely lived up to his reputation. Since then our paths have crossed multiple times on the conference circuit, and we have continued to collaborate through Whole School SEND. Rob's research expertise, alongside his knowledge of the SEND community and his ability to bring together a diverse range of perspectives, makes him ideally placed to edit this important book.

Whether you are personally or professionally motivated, this book provides a set of thoughtful reflective accounts of policy and practice. The current educational landscape is one where school funding is deemed by many to be insufficient, where both the number of pupils and the complexity of their needs are increasing, and where the recruitment and the retention of teachers are challenging. In such a context, the way in which we provide for our most vulnerable leaners speaks volumes about the views of society as a whole. Reading this book, you will find that the contributors shine a light on both past and present societal attitudes towards learners with SEND in addition to making suggestions about what the future may hold.

Unsurprisingly, a recurring principle across all of the chapters is the concept of inclusion. Or perhaps I should say the 'many concepts of inclusion' because, as this book demonstrates, there is no majority consensus on what inclusion really means. However, there does seem to be general agreement that inclusion is under threat, whichever definition is subscribed to. Indeed, the views of Baroness Warnock herself on the notion of inclusion and whether or not it is a good thing appear to have developed over time. This is evident in an illuminating discussion between Rob Webster and Baroness Warnock in which she reflects on the Enquiry and shares her current views (I should add that there is also a link to a video of the discussion, which is excellent!).

My own view of inclusion echoes that of nasen, which has been a champion, friend and protector of the SEND community for many years. In December 1991, the National Association for Remedial Education merged with the National Council for Special Education to form nasen. Essentially, this partnership saw a professional body for specialist provision merging with a professional body for mainstream provision. The merger was aligned to the principles of inclusion established by Baroness Warnock, which she reaffirms in this book. She is clear that she believes both specialist settings and mainstream schools have a role to play in an inclusive education system.

In conclusion, this is a timely book that will be both interesting and informative for new and experienced members of the SEND community. In a constructive sense, I found that it supported some of my own views but also made me question others, which is an important aspect of critical self-reflection. The contributors in this book are all well-respected members of the SEND community in their own right, and so credit must go to Rob Webster for bringing together such a diverse and thought-provoking set of perspectives within one tome. This is a book that will be at the top of my reading list for some time to come.

Note

1 Whole School SEND is a consortium of organisations delivering the SEND schools' workforce development programme for the Department for Education.

Contributor biographies

Dr Maggie Atkinson
CEO, Maggie Atkinson Consulting Ltd., and former Children's Commissioner for England

Maggie Atkinson has had a 40-year career, working to level the playing field for children who cannot level it for themselves. Her work as a teacher, trainer, adviser and inspector, as Gateshead's Director of Education and Culture (2003–2005) and of all its Children's Services (2005–2010), focussed on ensuring that children who needed better chances and services got them. Maggie was President of the Association of Directors of Children's Services (ADCS) (2008–2009) and wrote and published the government's all-agencies Children's 2020 Workforce Strategy. In 2010–2015, she was England's Children's Commissioner, promoting and protecting the rights of the child, particularly for those most vulnerable. She holds an EdD from Keele, where she is now an Honorary Professor, and she has Honorary Doctorates from the Universities of Northumbria, Keele and Nottingham Trent. She is a Trustee of the Michael Sieff Foundation. The Foundation's theme for 2018/19 is children and young people with SEND, with particular regard to those with Education, Health and Care Plans.

Dr Adam Boddison
Chief Executive, National Association of Special Educational Needs (nasen)

Dr Adam Boddison is the Chief Executive for nasen, with responsibility for strategic direction and operational delivery across the full breadth of nasen's activity. He is also the Chair of the Whole School SEND consortium, which is leading on the delivery of the government's SEND Schools' Workforce contract. Adam is a National Leader of Governance; Chair and Vice-Chair of two local authority primary schools; and a Trustee at two multi-academy trusts, which span primary, secondary and specialist settings. He is a Trustee of the Potential Trust, a member of the National SEND Forum and a Fellow of the RSA. Prior to joining nasen, he was Director of the Centre for Professional Education at the University of Warwick and Academic Principal for the International Gateway for Gifted Youth (IGGY), a global educational social network for gifted teenagers.

Ruth Cigman

Honorary Senior Research Associate, UCL Institute of Education

Ruth Cigman has a PhD in philosophy of music from the University of Cambridge and taught philosophy in the USA for several years before becoming a lecturer at UCL, first at the Medical School, then at the IOE. She has published widely in medical ethics and philosophy of education, and commissioned and edited Mary Warnock's *Special Educational Needs: A New Look* (2005) as well as a follow-up volume (with a foreword by Mary Warnock) called *Included or Excluded? The Challenge of the Mainstream for Some SEN Children.* Ruth recently published *Cherishing and the Good Life of Learning: Ethics, Education, Upbringing* (2018). In addition to working in academia, she runs The Cotton Tree Trust, a charity for refugees and asylum seekers in London.

Tara Flood

Director, Alliance for Inclusive Education (ALLFIE)

Tara Flood has been involved with the disability rights movement at a grass-roots level for many years. Since 2006, she has been the Director of ALLFIE, which campaigns for the right of all disabled pupils and students to be included in mainstream education and for ending segregation. Tara works with organisations led by disabled people, allied organisations, children's rights organisations, statutory agencies and government departments, both in a personal and in a professional capacity. She was involved in the discussions at the United Nations (UN) in the development of the UN Convention on the Rights of Persons with Disabilities, and she is now working to get the Convention fully implemented. Tara is committed to creating social and political change that will deliver equality for all disabled people at all levels and ensuring that the voices and experiences of all disabled people are at the heart of discussions and decision-making about our lives.

Nancy Gedge
Teacher, trainer and writer

Nancy Gedge is an experienced teacher, trainer and qualified special educational needs coordinator. She manages a resource base for pupils with physical disabilities and autism at a secondary school in Oxfordshire. Her experience in relation to SEND is not limited to school. Her eldest child has severe and profound learning difficulties: Down's syndrome. Nancy is an award-winning writer and won the *Tes* 'Teacher Blogger of the Year' award in 2015 for her blog *The Diary of a Not So Ordinary Boy*. Her first book, *Inclusion for Primary School Teachers*, was published in 2016. She is the SEND columnist for *Tes*.

Vic Goddard
Principal, Passmores Academy

Vic Goddard is probably the most famous head teacher in the UK today. He came to the public's attention in television's *Educating Essex*. Since then, his straight-talking, informal, light-hearted approach has meant that some sections of the media have misunderstood what he is really all about: refusing to ever let a student fail. Vic is passionate about young people, about education and about the privileged position he holds. His book, *The Best Job in the World*, perfectly describes his view on headship. Vic commands respect, not because of what he is but because of how he treats everyone around him: with compassion, with relentlessly high expectations and with an infectious belief that we all have something to offer the world.

Dr Alan Hodkinson
Associate Professor, Centre for Culture and Disability Studies, Faculty of Education, Liverpool Hope University

Alan Hodkinson was formerly a teacher of children labelled as SEND and is now an Associate Professor of learning support in schools at Liverpool Hope University. His research interests include the representations of impairment and disability in textbooks and digital media employed within educational settings, and national and international policy and practice formulation in relation to educational inclusion and special educational needs.

Peter Imray
Trainer, advisor and writer

Peter Imray is a freelance trainer, advisor and writer in the area of special educational needs. His current interests centre on pedagogy, curriculum and assessment relating to severe learning difficulties (SLD) and profound and multiple learning difficulties (PMLD). Peter is a Trustee of Equals, a UK not-for-profit charity working with and for children, young people and adults with SLD and PMLD. He is also a regular blogger on the SLD Forum and has written numerous articles for various journals. Peter is co-author (with Viv Hinchcliffe) of *Curricula for Teaching Children and Young People with Severe and Profound and Multiple Learning Difficulties*. His new book, *Inclusion is Dead: Long Live Inclusion*, written with Andrew Colley, is a polemic against the dominant inclusive ideology of a common school and/or class and/or curriculum for those with SLD and PMLD. It was published by Routledge in 2017.

Brahm Norwich
Professor of Educational Psychology and Special Educational Needs, Graduate School of Education, University of Exeter

Brahm Norwich's current research projects focus on lesson study, targeted interventions using a class organisation model and national trends in the placement of pupils with SEN. He is also interested in theoretical issues about the nature of special needs and inclusive education, having published books and papers on these and many other areas. Brahm's recent publications include Norwich, B. (2017) *Experiencing Special Educational Needs: Lessons for Practice* and Norwich, B. and Koutsouris, G. (2017) 'Addressing dilemmas and tensions in inclusive education', in *Oxford Research Encyclopaedia of Education: Education, Change, and Development*. DOI: 10.1093/acrefore/9780190264093.013.154

Vijita Patel
Principal, Swiss Cottage School

Vijita Patel is the Principal of Swiss Cottage School, Development and Research Centre, a special needs school for children aged 2–19 in the London borough of Camden. The school is a designated National Teaching School, leading an alliance of schools, organisations and higher education partners to provide teacher training and support school improvement priorities across the region and country. Swiss Cottage is one of eight schools in the country to have achieved six consecutive 'Outstanding' Ofsted Inspections. As a National Leader of Education, Vijita supports head teachers, senior and middle leaders, SEND coordinators, and local authorities on leading locality and provision developments. She has contributed to the development of programmes for teacher training and leadership development, and worked with postgraduate students on personalised learning through research on cognitive processing. Vijita is also a Trustee for the Varkey Foundation and Swiss Cottage School Charity.

Sally Phillips
Award-winning writer and actress

Sally Phillips is well known for her roles in *Smack the Pony*, *Miranda* and *The Green Wing*, and the *Bridget Jones* trilogy. Now an established face in British comedy and film, she began her career at the Edinburgh Festival Fringe when she was just 18. Sally got her big break in 1997 in *I'm Alan Partridge*, for which she was nominated Best Female Newcomer at the British Comedy Awards. Sally fronted, and was heavily involved in, a BBC documentary called *A World Without Down's Syndrome?*, which explored a new screening test that claims to detect Down's syndrome in pregnancy. As a result, Sally was nominated for a National Diversity Award in 2016. The documentary has been screened around the world; it was shortlisted for the 2017 Grierson Awards and won two Sandford St Martins Awards: for the Best Ethical Programme and the *Radio Times* Award for reader's choice.

Jon Severs
Commissioning Editor, *Tes*

Jon Severs has been Commissioning Editor at *Tes* since 2013. Previously, he wrote for publications as diverse as *Local Government News*, *Amateur Photographer*, *The Independent* and *The Grocer*. At *Tes* he commissions all features content for online and print, helping teachers stay informed about the latest educational research while facilitating the sharing of great classroom and leadership practice. He also runs the *Tes Podagogy* podcast, where academics provide insights into key educational topic areas. He visits around 30 schools per year minimum, across the UK and the education sectors.

Baroness Mary Warnock CH DBE FBA FMedSci
Baroness Mary Warnock taught philosophy at St Hugh's College, Oxford, from 1949 to 1966. Thanks to two books on existentialism in the 1960s, she became a regular commentator on philosophy on BBC Radio 3. She served as headmistress of the Oxford High School from 1966 to 1972 and as a member of the Independent Broadcasting Authority from 1973 to 1983. Mary was mistress of Girton College, Cambridge, from 1984 to 1991. She became a life peer in 1985, taking the title Baroness Warnock of

Weeke. She is perhaps best known for chairing two national committees of enquiry, each of which published a significant report. The first enquiry reported on the education of children and young people with special educational needs and disabilities (1978). The second enquiry, *A Question of Life: The Warnock Report on Human Fertilisation and Embryology* (1984), dealt with the ethics of embryos and human fertilisation. Mary's extensive writing includes published works on ethics, existentialism and the philosophy of Jean-Paul Sartre. Her memoir, *Mary Warnock: A Memoir – People and Places,* was published in 2000.

Paul Warren

Paul Warren has worked in further education and adult community education for over 14 years. He has a keen interest in the effective deployment of learning support staff as well as the use of technology to enable learners with physical and learning disabilities and difficulties. He is a strong advocate for self-empowerment techniques, such as growth mindset, grit and resilience. He currently manages a small independent vinyl record label.

Rob Webster

Associate Professor, Centre for Inclusive Education, UCL Institute of Education

Rob Webster has been researching in the field of inclusion and special educational needs for 15 years. Between 2011 and 2017, he conducted a longitudinal cohort study focussing on the educational experiences of pupils with SEND in mainstream and special schools. Taken together, the Making a Statement and the SEN in Secondary Education studies represent the UK's largest observational study of pupils with SEND. Rob has a specific interest in the role of teaching assistants. He worked on the groundbreaking Deployment and Impact of Support Staff project, and his extensive writing on this topic includes numerous journal articles and two acclaimed books: *Maximising the Impact of Teaching Assistants* and *The Teaching Assistant's Guide to Effective Interaction.* Rob currently leads the Maximising the Impact of Teaching Assistants initiative, which includes a randomised control trial, funded by the Education Endowment Foundation.

Klaus Wedell CBE HonFBPsS

Former Chair in Special Education, UCL Institute of Education

Klaus Wedell was an educational psychologist in Bristol and Hull. After academic posts at the University of Birmingham, he was appointed in

1979 to the first chair in Special Education at the Institute of Education, London. He was responsible for investigating the implementation of the Education Act 1981 and participated in two post-Warnock reviews of special educational needs for the National Children's Bureau (1984) and the Inner London Education Authority (1985). Klaus has consulted on special needs in Britain and overseas. On his retirement in 1995, he co-founded the National SEND Coordinators' Forum, an online support network. Currently, Klaus is the special needs governor for his village school and helps as a part-time voluntary teaching assistant.

Andria Zafirakou
Teacher, Alperton Community School, and Global Teacher Prize Winner 2018

Andria Zafirakou teaches art and textiles at Alperton Community School, a secondary school in the London borough of Brent. She learned the basics of many of the 35 languages spoken at Alperton as part of her efforts to earn the trust of marginalised students and establish relationships with their parents. Her determination to move beyond an identikit school curriculum has seen Alperton awarded UCL Institute of Education's Professional Development Platinum Mark – an honour that fewer than ten British schools have achieved. In March 2018, Andria became the first-ever UK winner of the Varkey Foundation's Global Teacher Prize. She is investing her $1m prize money into Artists in Residence, a programme to promote the importance of arts in education, and to inspire young people to pursue careers in the arts, by giving schools unparalleled access to time with leading artists.

Editor's introduction

Over the 2017/18 academic year, UCL Institute of Education (IOE), in association with *Tes*, the UK's long-standing publication for the teaching profession, held a series of public debates. Each debate brought together a range of commentators – academics, campaigners, practitioners, policy experts and others – and challenged them to bring fresh thinking to apparently intractable issues within the English education system.

The event, held on a sunny evening in May 2018 at the IOE – *'What if... we thought anew about how we support special educational needs and disability in our schools?'*[1] – was scheduled to coincide with the 40th anniversary of the publication of *The Report of the Committee of Enquiry into the Education of Handicapped Children and Young People*. This milestone provided a timely opportunity to not only recognise the achievements of the Warnock Report, as it is more memorably known, but also to reflect on the status quo and, further, to consider how we might address and resolve the persistent problems relating to inclusion and the education of children and young people with special educational needs and disability (SEND).

The idea for this book was developed from the IOE SEND debate. As well as formally capturing the views and experiences of the panellists, this book widens the debate by bringing to it a greater number of voices, perspectives and expertise. Contributors were invited to respond to one or both questions in the title of this book: how far have we come since the Warnock Enquiry, and where do we go next? The purpose of this book is not to provide a heavyweight dissection of the Warnock Enquiry itself but to explore aspects of the conceptional and practical territory of SEND and inclusion covered by the Warnock Committee. Accordingly, in some chapters, references to the enquiry and the 1978 report are more implicit.

The first chapter provides a short history of the purpose, contribution and impact of the Warnock Enquiry. We then hear from the enquiry's chair, Baroness Warnock, in the form of an interview conducted in March 2018. Thereafter, we come to the contributions that form the body of this book, starting with the experiences of Paul Warren, who, as a child with (as he puts it) 'so-called "SEND"' growing up in the 1970s, experienced the education system that the Warnock Enquiry aimed to improve. Subsequent chapters from practitioners, researchers, campaigners, parents of young people with SEND and others provide individual perspectives on the Warnock Report and its legacy. We conclude with précis of some important trends in English education in relation to SEND and, by drawing on the contributions to this book, offer up some suggestions for what could be done to ensure there is no slipping back on the inclusion agenda.

A note on terms

UK readers might be aware that 'inquiry', rather than 'enquiry', is more commonly used for formal or official investigations, of which the review led by Baroness Warnock is a prime example. In practice, these words are used interchangeably; indeed, the text of the Warnock Report does precisely this. For the purposes of consistency, however, this book uses the latter spelling throughout, simply because this is the one used in the full title of the Warnock Report.

Elsewhere, I have chosen not to standardise references to 'special educational needs' and 'disabilities', with some contributors preferring to refer to SEN, some preferring to refer to just disability, others preferring to refer to SEN *and* disability, and others still preferring to refer to SEN/D – implying that those with SEN may or may not have disabilities too, and vice versa. For the most part, the reader can assume that what applies to one constituency also applies in large part to the other. On a similar note, references to 'children' can be taken to include young people.

Note

1 To watch a video of the UCL IOE SEND debate, visit https://www.ucl. ac.uk/ioe/news-events/events-pub/may-2018/what-if-special-educational-needs-disability, or https://youtu.be/Jc_W9T6oHa4. For more information on the IOE Debates series, visit https://www.ucl.ac.uk/ioe/news-events/public-debates.

1 Looking back

A brief history of the Warnock Enquiry

Rob Webster

The significance of *The Report of the Committee of Enquiry into the Education of Handicapped Children and Young People* is evident from its first paragraph.

> Ours was the first committee of enquiry specifically charged by any government of the United Kingdom to review educational provision for all handicapped children, whatever their handicap. The last such body to have terms of reference which approached our own in breadth was the Royal Commission on the Blind, the Deaf and Dumb and Others of the United Kingdom which reported in 1889.
>
> (Section 1.1)

While commissions since the late nineteenth century have reported on specific disabilities and conditions, it would be 85 years before the UK government undertook as expansive a review into special education as the 1889 enquiry. Adopting the name of its chair, Mary Warnock, the enquiry commenced in 1974 and published its final report in May 1978.

The Warnock Enquiry remains the most comprehensive review of special educational needs and disabilities (SEND) ever commissioned by a UK government. Members of its committee visited every type of setting: mainstream schools; nurseries; special nursery units; state, independent and residential special schools; further education (FE) colleges; assessment centres; hospitals; teacher training colleges; and departments of education in universities. It reached beyond the UK, investigating provisions in Canada, the USA, Sweden, Denmark and the Netherlands. The enquiry's themes ranged from categorisations of SEND, education within and across settings, relationships between families, health and social services, research in universities and teacher training.

A change in the law

In November 1971, a Labour backbencher asked the then secretary of state for education and science, Margaret Thatcher, to consider an enquiry into 'the whole field of special education'. The minister declined: 'I do not think that this would be helpful in present circumstances' (HC Deb 825, 1971). Three years later, the proponent of that request, Doris Fisher, tried again. This time, Mrs Thatcher agreed. 'I believe', she said, 'that the time is ripe for a general enquiry which will go somewhat beyond the specifically educational needs of the handicapped' (HC Deb 864, 1973).

The lady, it seemed, *was* for turning. Yet it was not so much Mrs Thatcher's mind that had changed but the law. Legislation following the Education (Handicapped Children) Act 1970 meant that all children and young people were required to attend school. Yet little was known about the appropriate environments for those deemed by many, for so long, to be 'ineducable'.

Both the 1970 Act and the appointment of the Warnock Enquiry reflected maturing social attitudes to disability. Over the 1950s, parent-led pressure groups began pushing back against the pervasive – and limiting – notion of ineducability. As Mary Warnock describes in Chapter 2 of this book, an influential figure over this period was Stanley Segal, 'a highly energetic' head teacher of a London special school. Segal lobbied members of Parliament by mobilising special educators' and parents' knowledge and experiences of the learning capabilities of 'mentally handicapped' children. He robustly challenged the long-standing and pessimistic notion that 'the mentally defective were somehow a different species or were both abnormal as well as subnormal, and a matter for doctors rather than teachers' (Segal, 1967). Greater awareness of the interaction between within-child factors and environmental factors informed a shared understanding of what children with physical disabilities and/or learning difficulties could and could not do.

Over the same period, epidemiological studies of educational, psychiatric and physical disorders in 9- to 11-year-old children, conducted on the Isle of Wight (Rutter *et al.*, 1970), provided evidence that around 20 per cent of children were likely to have special educational needs at some point in their school career, which would require some form of special education provision. While additional estimates from the time suggested between 1.8 per cent and 2 per cent of the school population had severe, complex and long-term needs, the 'one in five' figure assumed educational, political and administrative significance.

This, together with new understandings about disability, led to a paradigmatic shift in perception, which, in turn, paved the way for both more open and applied practices in special education and the legislative change that would bolster and amplify it.

A new vision

The Warnock Enquiry's terms of reference were:

> To review educational provision in England, Scotland and Wales for children and young people handicapped by disabilities of body or mind, taking account of the medical aspects of their needs, together with arrangements to prepare them for entry into employment; to consider the most effective use of resources for these purposes; and to make recommendations.

As noted earlier, the terms went 'beyond the specifically educational needs of the handicapped', and its subsequent recommendations implicated professionals in health and social care as well as education. The committee's report and recommendations reflected the hard-won right of people with disabilities to 'uninhibited participation in the activities of everyday life, in all their varied forms' (Section 7.1). Warnock invokes a description of 'integration' taken from the Snowdon Working Party (1976), and which, while written with people with physical disabilities in mind, captured 'the spirit of changing attitudes to handicap in all its manifestations':

> Integration for the disabled means a thousand things. It means the absence of segregation. It means social acceptance. It means being able to be treated like everybody else, it means the right to work, to go to cinemas, to enjoy outdoor sport, to have a family life and a social life and a love life, to contribute materially to the community, to have the usual choices of association, movement and activity, to go on holiday to the usual places, to be educated up to university level with one's un-handicapped peers, to travel without fuss on public transport...
>
> (Section 7.1)

The Warnock Report is sometimes credited as introducing inclusion, but in reality, it was a catalyst. 'The principle is not new to education', states the introduction to the chapter, 'Special education in ordinary schools'. 'It had been long-standing government policy, confirmed in numerous official documents, that no child should be sent to a special school who can be satisfactorily educated in an ordinary one' (Section 7.2). As such, the committee's report contained no new or original recommendations relating to the law on integration or inclusion. It did, however, set out a coherent case for improving the quality of special education and for more inclusive, less segregational, forms of schooling that embodied social acceptance. While integration implies a sense of pupils adapting to the school, the committee's vision required schools to do the adjusting.

The Warnock Report

The Warnock Report consolidated and brought together many different strands of thinking and practice in special education and employment in one place, and articulated a cohesive and expansive plan for lifelong inclusion for those with SEND. Special schools and 'ordinary' (i.e. mainstream) schools would be brought closer together. Special units attached to, and functioning as part of, mainstream schools would facilitate 'locational' and 'social' integration (Sections 7.7–7.8). Young people would be supported to attend 'ordinary' courses at FE colleges. Universities and polytechnics were advised to develop admissions policies for students with SEND. Industrial Training Boards were to encourage employers to provide employment and training opportunities for people with disabilities or significant difficulties. And there was a call for more opportunities for people with disabilities to become teachers.

The enquiry was pre-eminently about the quality of special education, but as Warnock acknowledges early on in the report, quality 'cannot be guaranteed merely by legislation and structural change'. The framework outlined in the report's 220 recommendations provided 'the setting within which people work together in the interests of children, and the quality of education depends essentially upon their skill and insight, backed by adequate resources — not solely educational resources — efficiently deployed' (Section 2.85).

Accordingly, a significant aspect of the report focussed on teachers and the wider network of professionals working with children and young people with special needs, and their families. The substantive chapter entitled 'Teacher education and training' recognised that increasing teachers' knowledge of SEND was 'of the utmost importance'. While in-service training was 'vital', Warnock argued that 'the groundwork should be laid in initial training'. The committee recommended that a 'special education element' be included in all initial teacher education courses 'as soon as possible' (Sections 21.1–12.10).

Warnock envisaged a new special education workforce developing up around teachers to support and facilitate. Universities and teacher training colleges would require 'at least 200 additional full-time lecturers' to deliver the special education element (Section 12.14). Mainstream head teachers were required to appoint a 'designated specialist teacher' who would assume 'day-to-day responsibility for making arrangements for children with special needs' (Section 7.28). The first indications of the creation of a paraprofessional workforce are also evident in the committee's report. It called for the appointment of at least one ancillary worker (or non-teaching assistant) to work in special classes and units attached to mainstream schools (Section 14.32).

Across several further chapters, the report made recommendations concerning the roles of a cadre of practitioners who interact with children with special needs and their families beyond school, in educational psychology, careers, social services, health and medicine. Warnock stressed the requirement for a much closer coordination between these services. There were even suggestions relating to interprofessional training between disciplines that could lead to dual qualifications, such as in health and psychology. Much of what Warnock proposed regarding initial teacher training (ITT) and collaborative multi-agency working remains unresolved. Contributors to this book examine some of these missed opportunities and failings.

Introducing 'special educational needs'

One of the enquiry's most significant achievements was transforming how we talk about disability. It provided the first major challenge to the medical model of disability: where impairments and differences are portrayed as intrinsic to the individual and the cause of disadvantage and lower quality of life. The medical model had been sustained over decades by the terminology used to officially categorise people with learning difficulties and disabilities. The Mental Deficiency Act 1913 required local education boards to identify 'mentally defective' children and young people aged 7–16 and categorise them on the basis of their IQ as 'idiots', 'imbeciles' or 'feeble-minded'. Under the Education Act 1944, many children with SEND were considered 'uneducable' and grouped, again by IQ, into categories such as 'maladjusted' or 'educationally subnormal'. Limiting and dehumanising language like 'backward' and 'retarded' were commonplace (Wood, 1929).

Warnock concluded that such labels were not just unhelpful for identifying an individual's educational needs but amounted to a life sentence. The enquiry popularised the term 'special educational needs', conceived by Ronald Gulliford (1971), and consigned the most pernicious labels to history. Conceptualisations of special educational needs were widened in ways that made it clearer to teachers that they would have some pupils with SEND in their classrooms.

The Education Act 1981

Though the Warnock Enquiry was initiated by Edward Heath's Conservative government, the committee undertook its work during the Labour governments of Harold Wilson and James Callaghan (1974–1978). Labour dithered in its response to the final report, and 12 months after it was published, the Conservatives, now led by Margaret Thatcher, returned to power. The committee's recommendations then found a legislative home in the 1981 Education Act.

The Act introduced the system of statutory assessment – or 'statementing'. Although the requirement for the secretary of state to issue a code of practice of practical guidance came later, with the Education Act 1993, there were key elements of the basic statementing machinery, proposed by the Warnock Committee, that have endured, including parents' right to appeal decisions made by the local authority (Section 4.74). What is more, elements of the 2014 SEND reforms were presaged by Warnock's recommendations. For example, the notion that provision and services should extend to the age of 25 (Section 16.31) and the requirement for councils to maintain an 'up-to-date handbook of local special education provision' (Section 6.15) – a nascent 'local offer'.

By the time the 1981 Act was implemented, the Conservative government had introduced a market-style approach to public services management, based on principles of individualism, competition and efficiency. There was, then, a marked difference in the social, political and economic contexts in which the report's recommendations would be enacted from that which prevailed when the committee was set up less than a decade earlier. As Lunt (2007) notes, this introduced 'a bleak contradiction between the aspirations of the report and the subsequent legislation'. The operational siloing and poor lateral working that are features of this approach to public administration are perhaps a reason why, as Mary Warnock describes in Chapter 2 of this book, multi-agency working has been so difficult to achieve.

Warnock reconsiders

Thirty years after the enquiry, Baroness Warnock (she was made a life peer in 1985) famously began estranging herself from the report's recommendations, calling for further moves towards inclusion to be resisted (Warnock, 2005). Ruth Cigman (2007), who worked with Mary Warnock on her 2005 pamphlet '*Special educational needs: A new look*', claims that the media's characterisation of this as a U-turn was 'politics', 'a response to a phrase... which had been subjected to the soundbite treatment'.

Warnock's (2007) concerns lay in criticisms of the framework of provision that had been put in place since the 1981 Education Act. This framework, she concluded, 'was failing some children disastrously'. Calling for the government to set up a committee of enquiry to 'consider the case for radical reform', Warnock argued that the need for a review hinged on two issues. The first was inconsistences relating to the issuing of Statements, a process consumed by bureaucracy and litigation, starved of funding and perpetually at risk of collapsing under the weight of its own contradictions (Shaw, 2003; Warnock, 2017). The second issue was the 'commitment to including in mainstream schools all those children whose parents wanted it, and many whose parents did not, regardless of the nature of their needs' (Warnock, 2007).

Warnock (2007) realised that while some mainstream schools were able to make the kinds of installational adjustments needed to accommodate pupils with SEND – to have them on-site and in classrooms – they had proved largely incapable of making the adaptations required to turn themselves into 'an environment in which such children can learn':

> However tolerant and supportive the policies, and however understanding the members of staff, there are limits to what realistically can be achieved in mainstream schools, given the diversity of children's needs and the finite available resources.

Moving on

The vision of a system where schools adjust to pupils with SEND, which underpinned the notion of inclusion at the heart of the Warnock Report, has yet to materialise. Whether this vision will ever be realised – and if so, how it might be achieved – is a key theme of the contributions to this book. As she explains in Chapter 2, Mary Warnock is not optimistic. For her, the group of children and young people hardest done by present arrangements are those with autistic spectrum conditions. For them, she says, '"inclusion" is a nightmare' (Warnock, 2007).

Many books, papers and articles have been written in the last four decades about where the Warnock Enquiry, and the legislation that followed, failed. Yet it would be a mistake to let these criticisms dictate the terms of its legacy. The work of the committee deserves credit for catalysing a fundamental shift in discourse on special needs and disability, banishing the concept of ineducability and tackling policies of segregation. Furthermore, we must acknowledge that the ambitions and actions related to inclusion do not exist separately from, nor are they insulated from, wider political and economic forces. Any indictment of the enquiry's underachievement has to be viewed within the context of the broader factors that directly and indirectly determined its implementation and its likely success.

In July 2018, 40 years after the publication of the report, Baroness Warnock (at the age of 94) addressed the first evidence session of the Education Committee's SEND enquiry. She pointed out that 1981, the year of the Education Act, 'was the very worst year for finances' (HC 968, 2018). Local authorities and schools began to experience financial pressure from the 'tremendous Thatcher cuts':

> It was a disastrous year for the Act to come out, because right from the start, it became clear that there were going to be far more financial pressures than we in our innocence had thought when we published the report in 1978. It really was from that moment on that things started to go wrong, entirely for financial reasons, not for conceptual reasons.

The parallel between Warnock's brief appraisal and the circumstances surrounding the development and roll-out of the Children and Families Act 2014 hardly needs comment. The fact that MPs in 2018 questioned Warnock about her enquiry is more evidence of why the 1978 report continues to resonate and have relevance today.

The SEND enquiry, launched in April 2018, and ongoing at the time of writing, 'is intended to review the success of [the 2014] reforms, how they have been implemented, and what impact they are having in meeting the challenges faced by children and young people with special educational needs and disabilities' (Education Committee, 2018). Producing far-reaching recommendations is not within its terms of reference. The fatigue created by the implementation of recent SEND reforms and, indeed, across the education sector as a whole – and which will doubtless be exposed through the enquiry – is likely to temper any recommendations the committee does produce. In any event, the political turbulence and biting austerity that has defined the 2010s, and which will define the policy context for the foreseeable future, stands in contrast to the experience that Warnock described earlier. Unlike in the mid-1970s, both the appetite for wholesale reform to the SEND system and the funds to bankroll it are in historically short supply.

In any event, we should not be seeking to emulate or replace the Warnock Report but to move it on. This book is as much a recognition of the report's significance and achievements 40 years on as it is a reminder of, and stimulus for, the need to continue debating its key ideas and principles, and to consider what inclusion ought to look like in the coming years and decades. By looking back, we might be better able to chart our way forward.

References

Cigman, R. (2007) 'Editorial introduction', in R. Cigman (ed.) *Included or excluded? The challenge of the mainstream for some SEN children.* Oxon: Routledge.

Education Committee (2018) *Special educational needs and disabilities inquiry launched.* Available online: www.parliament.uk/business/committees/ committees-a-z/commons-select/education-committee/news-parliament-2017/special-educational-needs-and-disability-launch-17-19/. Accessed on: 17 August 2018.

Gulliford, R. (1971) *Special educational needs.* London: Routledge and Kegan Paul.

HC 968 (2018) *Education Committee. Oral evidence: Special educational needs and Disabilities.* Available online: http://data.parliament.uk/writtenevidence/committeeevidence.svc/evidencedocument/education-committee/ special-educational-needs-and-disabilities/oral/86526.pdf. Accessed on: 17 August 2018.

HC Deb (22 November 1973) vol. 864 cols. 511–2W. Available online: http:// hansard.millbanksystems.com/written_answers/1973/nov/22/handicapped-children#S5CV0864P0_19731122_CWA_313. Accessed on: 17 August 2018.

HC Deb (9 November 1971) vol. 825 col. 140W. Available online: http://hansard. millbanksystems.com/written_answers/1971/nov/09/special-education# S5CV0825P0_19711109_CWA_186. Accessed on: 17 August 2018.

Lunt, I. (2007) 'The challenge of meeting additional educational needs with or without statements of special educational needs', in R. Cigman (ed.) *Included or excluded? The challenge of the mainstream for some SEN children.* Oxon: Routledge.

Rutter, M., Tizard, J. and Whitmore, K. (eds.) (1970) *Education, health and behaviour.* London: Longman.

Segal, S.S. (1967) *No child is ineducable. Special education – provision and trends.* London: Pergamon Press.

Snowdon Working Party (1976) *Integrating the disabled. Report of the Snowdon working party.* London: The National Fund for Research into Crippling Diseases.

Shaw, M. (2003) 'Warnock calls for rethink'. *TES*. Available online: www.tes. com/news/tes-archive/tes-publication/warnock-calls-rethink. Accessed on: 17 August 2018.

Warnock, M. (2017) 'Everything has changed... but nothing has changed'. *TES*. Available online: www.tes.com/news/tes-magazine/tes-magazine/ everything-has-changed-nothing-has-changed. Accessed on: 17 August 2018.

Warnock, M. (2007) 'Foreword', in. R. Cigman (ed.) *Included or excluded? The challenge of the mainstream for some SEN children.* Oxon: Routledge.

Warnock, M. (2005) *Special educational needs: A new look.* London: Philosophy of Education Society of Great Britain.

Wood, A.H. (1929) *Report of the Mental Deficiency Committee. A Joint Committee of the Board of Education and Board of Control.* London: HMSO. Available online: www.educationengland.org.uk/documents/wood/index. html. Accessed on: 17 August 2018.

2   Interview with Baroness Mary Warnock

This chapter is a transcript of an interview with Baroness Mary Warnock, conducted by the editor of this book, and recorded on 23 March 2018.[1]

How did you come to be involved in the committee of enquiry into special education?

Well, I don't really know, but I was already I think on the sort of list of people who are considered for jobs of this kind, because I'd been on a south-east planning committee before, so my name was sort of on the list. And I think, I suppose, because I'd been the headmistress of a school I was thought to be interested in education, interested in schools. Now I think that's how it came about, but I knew absolutely nothing about special education at all. The school that I was head of was a highly academic school, and it was complete news to me, the whole thing. So, I came with perhaps a useful ignorance of the whole subject.

What were attitudes towards disability and learning difficulties like at the time you were conducting the review [the mid-1970s] within the education system and wider society?

It was assumed by most people, especially people who knew very little about it, that the handicapped went to special schools. And it was taken for granted I think by most people that that was how things were and how things probably would stay. But the reason why the committee was set up, was that in the early seventies there was a highly energetic headteacher of a special school, called Segal. And he decided that nothing like enough was being done particularly for severely handicapped children. His school was for severely handicapped children. He started lobbying MPs and he wrote a book, which he handed out to all MPs, called *No child is ineducable*. Because up to 1972 there were children deemed ineducable and didn't go to school at all. They may, if they were lucky, have gone to a sort of workshop or that kind of thing, but they didn't go to school. So, the reason why Margaret Thatcher set up this committee as secretary of state for education, was simply because the law had changed. And now suddenly all children were going to go to school, and so she thought rightly that the whole situation therefore needed to be rethought. So that's why the Committee was started. And as I say, I think I was there because I knew something about schools, not because knew anything about disability.

Did you find that an advantage, not knowing anything about the field?

Yes, I think it's always an advantage if you haven't got a position of your own. You learn as you go along. And, therefore, you're open minded about what the outcome is going to be. I think that is quite an advantage. And, of course, it's very much the reason why philosophers are quite often appointed to this kind of position, because in a way they don't have a subject matter. They're hired, so to speak, to be open-minded and look at things from the beginning.

One of the achievements of the committee was to change the language around special needs and disabilities. Why was it important to review the official terminology that was in use at the time, such as 'educationally subnormal' and 'maladjusted'?

Well such vocabulary does change from time to time. I personally very much regretted the dropping of the word maladjusted, which is a rather specialist point in a way. But the psychiatrist who was a member of the committee, called Philip Graham, he too regretted the loss of the word maladjusted, because it both meant that the child was not capable of adjusting to school, but also that the school was not capable of adjusting to the child. So, I think that it was a useful term. But I suppose subnormal was thought to be a bit derogatory. The only thing was that we had to substitute for that, or did substitute for that, having learning difficulties, either mild or severe, and that's not really... that is a good word to apply to people at school, but in a way, it applied to all the children we were talking about. They all had learning difficulties. Some because they were deaf, some because they were blind and so on. So, it was not a terribly happy choice of words, I think, but I could never think of a better one.

The language changes, and there are consequences to any form of labelling. You challenge certain labels, like 'handicap' and 'educationally subnormal', but labels are also thought to be useful, particularly perhaps

by parents who are entering into the assessment system and the whole education process.

Yes, but of course, we constantly banged on about not labelling children. But, of course, you've got to refer to the children who have needs somehow or other. And I personally don't feel that it's in the least derogatory to say of somebody that she's blind. And it's terribly cumbersome the way one now has to talk about being visually impaired or auditorily impaired. It's all very awkward. And blind and deaf used to be perfectly good words to use, and did then. And after all, one uses it so constantly, metaphorically. I mean, nobody's going to say that you are visually impaired to my obvious needs! One needs to add blind and deaf. So, I think, deliberately changing the language was a bit silly really.

Do you think we are in the right place with the language at the moment? Are there any terms that you think might be problematic?

As I said, I like the word maladjusted. It seems to me useful. But, of course, maladjusted has been divided up into some of the other more complicated needs children are said to suffer from. So, I suppose, you would say the language has been refined, but I'm sure it'll change again one day.

What do you see as the most positive legacy of the Committee's work?

I think by far the most positive legacy was actually the one that was by far the most difficult to get across to people at the time. Because everybody thinks that what we said was that there must be inclusion; that children with special needs must be included in regular classrooms, mainstream classrooms. But in fact, at least part of what we were saying, if not more, was that in classes as they were constituted then, when we [the committee] were meeting, there was already a considerable number of children who we thought had special needs. So, it was not so much that we were going to bring in a whole lot of children who hadn't been into classrooms before – though that was part of it, of course – it was also, we were trying to point out that there already were these children in the classroom whom teachers must realise did have special needs. And that was a large part of what we meant by inclusion.

In the early 2000s, you started to express some dissatisfaction with the system the committee and the report helped to create. you singled out the statementing system, calling it 'disastrous'. What were you seeing and hearing that gave rise to these concerns?

Well, statementing had become entirely a matter of trying to get extra money. We decided, after some thought, that in our report, we weren't going to cost any of the things that we recommended, because we knew they'd be expensive and we knew that the costs won't stand still, and also, I knew that we'd spend an awful lot of time – we'd waste an awful lot of time if we talked about the costs of anything. So, we made this decision that we weren't going to cost it. And in a way this was wrong, I think, because what had gone wrong with statementing was that it became entirely a matter of finance. The original thought had been that the Statement would specify exactly what a particular child needed if he was going to flourish educationally, but in fact it turned out that the local authority put into the Statement whatever they could afford, and nothing else. So, the Statement was in two ways financially determined. One was that the local authority wouldn't say if a child needed, say, language therapy, or something of that kind, every day – as some children certainly did. They would say, once a week, because they thought they could afford that. But, on the other hand, the schools were very keen to get children Statements, because they got a bit of extra money thereby. So, the whole issue of what the child actually needed, which was meant to go into the Statement, had got sort of slurred over, and the Statement became really just a matter of what little bit of extra money people thought they could screw out of government. And that's why I said it was disastrous.

Last year (2017), writing in the TES, you were quite scathing of the new system of Education, Health and Care Plans (EHCPs), which have replaced Statements. What do you feel is going wrong, and what should we be doing differently?

Well, I was very cynical about them [EHCPs], because the most difficult, the greatest difficulty, that my committee had was to devise a way in which social workers, doctors and teachers would talk to one another about the needs of the child. Because all of them, in many cases, most cases, all of them had something to contribute. But it was the most difficult thing in the world just to bring them together. And we didn't solve that problem. And I remember vividly, we had a weekend in which social workers and teachers – not the medical profession, but those two: social workers and teachers – who really were incredibly important; they should talk to one another. We got them together for a weekend so that they could thrash out, try to produce a sort of plan, by which they could automatically talk to one another and trust one another, and so on. What happened was, the minute we entered the hotel, the social workers went into one room and the teachers went into another room. And they never talked to one another at all except in formal meetings. And we simply never found a way that we could ensure that they always passed on what was relevant information. In fact, they were very unwilling to do so. And the social workers particularly were sort of fanatical – just as the doctors were about confidentially. And the teachers were never thought to be proper recipients of really sometimes quite crucial information. So, in that way I think, our report might as well have never have been written. And so, I was cynical when this great new idea of the doctors and the social workers and the teachers all sitting around the table making this wonderful Plan. I knew it wasn't going to happen, because in fact, it was the teachers who were the ones that drew up the Plan – who do now draw up the Plan – and therefore the emphasis is still entirely on education, and not on either medicine or social needs.

What do you think the statementing process and the processes around the new EHCPs are doing to the aims of inclusion?

Well, that is a very interesting question, because I think quite separately, there are more people now who are dubious about inclusion. And we had on the committee people of varying degrees of enthusiasm for inclusion, and the people who were least in favour of inclusion, I think were myself and the member of the committee who was professor of adolescent psychiatry, because he knew perfectly well that there were some people who could disrupt a class by simply being there. And the other people who were not enthusiastic were people who knew about autism. We didn't have a specialist on autism on the committee, but as it happened, I knew a bit about autism myself, because I have a very severely autistic nephew. So, I knew what the needs of autistic pupils were, and emphatically they were not to be in a large class where people bashed into you and expected you to join in, and all that. So, I don't know... I think quite separately from abolishing Statements and having these Plans, quite separately from that, I think more people now are dubious about inclusion than they were. And I know that Michael Gove, when he was in charge of education, welcomed what he saw as new avoidance of being too enthusiastic about inclusion. And in that, I think he was absolutely right, because besides autistic children I think there are some very vulnerable children who flourish much better in a small school. I mean, they'd probably get on alright at primary school, which tend to be smaller and more relaxed, but once it gets to secondary school, I think there are quite a lot of children who are not autistic, but who actually find the sort of absolute hurly-burly of a huge school quite difficult to put up with.

In principle, should we strive for an education system that is fully inclusive, that does not have any special schools?

No. Absolutely not. I'm really again thinking of the people on the autistic spectrum, and Asperger's children as well. They really cannot put up with a large class and a large playground. And I've talked to a very large number of parents of autistic children – and I did in the beginning of the century when I wrote something about it – and I really think there's an unanimity that the autistic child does need a special school. And there they can, many of them, flourish.

If the government, be it a Labour government, or a Conservative government, or another government, announced a new enquiry into special education needs and disability, what do you think it should focus on?

I believe that it should focus on teacher training. And I know that teachers will probably think that I'm extraordinarily demanding in what I think they ought to do, but I really do believe that teachers must be trained in their attitude towards the pupils in their classes. Somehow, they've [the government] got to get teachers to realise that their job is enormously important. But it isn't a matter of conveying information to their pupils; it's a matter of loving them, quite frankly. They've got to really engage with their pupils. And actually, it's so easy to get information now; one's only got to one's computer and one can get masses of information. And the teacher can help the child sort out the information. But they don't really. Although, getting children to know things – know more than they do when they're very small – is obviously enormously important – an awful lot of their getting-to-know-things happens as much at home as at school. And the teacher's task is to engage with the pupils as people. And in that way, I think a lot of pupils would enjoy school much more than they do now. And the teachers would feel that their job is unique, and can't be done on the internet.

There is a considerable section in the 1978 report on the role of teaching training. You talk about the structures and the legislation that would be required for a new system, but do not leave out teacher training. You refer to it as being of 'the upmost importance', and recommend the integration of a 'special education element' into initial teacher training. And you make a comment in the report that says: 'Some 40 years will need to elapse from the time that the proposed special education element is introduced before it can be assumed that all teachers have undertaken such an element in the course of their initial training' [Section 12.12]. How do you

think the education system is doing on training teachers to know how to meet the needs of pupils with SEND?

I don't honestly know the answer to that question, because I'm not up to date with what teacher training is actually like. But my guess is that it doesn't give enough attention to the personal relationship that must hold between teachers and pupils. And I think it's fairly obvious that it's really very difficult to make a good teacher, but there are ways that it can be done. And I think it's much more likely to be done when the training is largely based in schools, as it is now, then it was when the trainee only went into a school for a very short time, and otherwise it was lectures from people who really hadn't been into school for donkey's years themselves probably. So, I think teacher training is in general better now that it's more school-focussed. And the trainee can really learn by doing and trying, which I think is excellent. But how much there is to enable the trainees to pick up how to make sure that everybody in the class is actually benefitting from what happens; that I think... well, it's difficult to quantify. But that's what ought to be the core of teacher training, I think. That they should constantly check on what connections they have – what their personal connections are – even with a class of 30. I just read an amazing book by somebody called Ruth Cigman, which has the word 'cherishing' in its title[2]. And she says that this is what teachers ought to cultivate in their relation with their pupils. And I like the word cherishing, because the word caring is now not the name of any emotional transaction, its simply the name of a profession, or something sometimes frequently done by amateurs. But it's a professional word, and it has no emotional content at all. But I think that loving their pupils is what the teacher has to be trained to do, and then they'll see as they go along who's floundering, who's in difficulties, who really does need a bit of extra help, even quite a little bit of extra help. And I think this is what should be the core of teacher training, and I'm not sure that it is.

So, you think there is a space for teaching to be a profession that shouldn't be afraid or should shy away from terms like 'cherish' and 'nurture' and 'love'?

Absolutely. Nurture is a very good word, because there are nurture groups in some schools, aren't there, and I think they're very, very good. They take the child out into a smaller group, and maybe they stay in this nurture group all the time, for two years or so. Maybe they stay for much less time; maybe they just drop in and out. But the fact that there are, within the school, small spaces where the whole point is to look after the child, to check up on him, make sure he's alright, that seems to me an excellent thing.

It's tempting to ask you where you think we might be in the next 40 years, but that seems a bit too far away. So, what about the next ten years? What do you think the challenges are in the school system in relation to SEND, and are there any grounds for optimism?

Well, I'm afraid, I already said I'm cynical about the interconnection between the professionals who are involved with children with special needs, and I'm afraid I'm still sceptical that there's going to be much change. It just is incredibly difficult to get the three professions involved, really to take one another seriously. Each one of them thinks that their own role in the bringing up of this child is the most important. I mean, that's good; professional should take themselves seriously. But I think it is very unlikely that things will dramatically change in the next ten years, I'm afraid. But I do hope, like Michael Gove, though we don't lose sight of the notion of inclusion, we don't concentrate on it too much. Because as I said before, it's not only autistic children, but it's them especially, for whom we need to do a lot more, I think.

But there might be some grounds for optimism with the teaching professional perhaps if we can inculcate a nurturing spirit?

Don't you agree that now there's so much information kicking around? I mean, I know a lot of it is false! [*laughs*]. I personally, being by no means a school child, nevertheless find it incredibly enlightening and useful that I can look things up on the internet so easily. I don't have to write down, as children used to have to do, lists of dates; I can just look it up. And I find that the most marvellous thing. And so, I'm very glad there's such easy access to information, but it does change the role of the teacher, I think. The teacher is there to guide the child how to get information sensibly. And otherwise, the teacher is incredibly important as one human being in contact with another. That's my view on the thing.

Notes

1 A video of the interview can be viewed online at https://youtube/tPZLFpxiQfw. An audio-only podcast version is available online: https://soundcloud.com/ioelondon/reflections-on-the-warnock-report-with-baroness-mary-warnock.
2 Cigman, R. (2018) *Cherishing and the good life of learning.* London: Bloomsbury Press.

3   Going to school in an ambulance

Paul Warren

Growing up as a child with so-called 'SEND' (special educational needs and disabilities) in the 1970s, during which time Baroness Warnock was conducting her enquiry, was highly challenging and profoundly difficult but surprisingly rewarding. Let me explain. My claim to being a disabled child came by virtue of a cocktail of neurological conditions: ataxic cerebral palsy, diagnosed in infancy, and an autistic spectrum *condition* (ASC) – for me, autism *is* a condition, not a 'disorder' – which was diagnosed in later life. The cerebral palsy was, apparently, 'mild'. I was often told my cerebral palsy was mild, almost always by people who did not have it themselves and who had no real idea whether it was mild or not. The cerebral palsy manifested itself in poor coordination (my fine motor skills are limited); my speech; and in difficulty with particular movements, including walking and running. The ASC, in hindsight, was responsible for my difficulties in forming friendships with other children and my fixation on topics such as classical music, outer space, dinosaurs, the Bible and foreign languages. My inability to take part in sports and other physical activities may have also contributed to the difficulties I experienced in forming relationships.

Fortunately, however, neither disability robbed me of one of the personal qualities I value most: my sense of humour. This has served me as a valuable asset throughout my life. Although it was often appreciated by many of my classmates, it also frequently got me into trouble with teachers who did not value my 'comic timing' as much!

Misunderstandings with teachers were not the only challenge I faced at school. By far the greatest difficulty was that almost every type of academic activity was assessed by a written exercise. Literacy was a challenge because I could hardly hold a pen, let alone write for long enough to complete the assessments to the required standard and in the allotted time. Using a ruler, a compass and a protractor meant mathematics was also demanding. Metalwork and woodwork similarly so. My junior school kindly purchased a state-of-the-art electronic typewriter for me in an attempt to help me speed up my work. Unfortunately, this well-meant intervention caused me more frustration than the problem it sought to resolve. My coordination difficulties and spatial awareness problems meant I could not hit the keys very well, and so typing proved a greater challenge than writing with a pen or a pencil.

A more radical solution to my learning problems had been proposed when I was around the age of nine. My mother suggested to me that I leave mainstream school and attend a 'special school' for children with various educational needs. Even at that young age, I somehow sensed that this would not be good for me, and I flatly declined. Not even the promise of going to school every day in a 'nice ambulance' could persuade me.

I was fortunate enough to have had the choice of where I went to school. Many other children did not have that choice, or they were unable to make that choice independently or articulate their view and make themselves heard as effectively as I was able to. While it was far from plain sailing, 'integration', as the Warnock Report described it, was the right option for me, but for many others, the mainstream system – with its tendency for a 'one size fits all' curriculum offer – was not even an option.

I transitioned to my local comprehensive school aged 11. My teachers recognised that despite my challenges, I was reasonably bright. I was put in the top set in my first year, but by the end of the year, I found myself in the bottom set due to increasing behavioural problems. I now recognise that my behaviour was a manifestation of my inability to keep up with the teacher or my peers. I stayed in the 'remedial' set for the remaining two years of secondary school.

Unfortunately, things continued to spiral downward. I left school with one O level (in French) and five very low-grade CSEs. Although I knew I could have done much better, the limitations of the curriculum imposed their own restrictions. There was only so much I could have achieved. So, in hindsight, I do not feel that I would have fared any better in a special school. The institutionalised approach that many schools of this nature took at that time would most probably have robbed me of the ability to experience the wider world.

On leaving school, I found it difficult to get a job in my home town. After two years, I had an assessment from the Disabled Resettlement Officer at the local job centre, which led to a referral to a skills centre in Bristol for people with disabilities. The skills centre assessment concluded that I was suited to administrative roles. I spent over 15 years doing clerical work, much of which required using a computer. Unlike the electronic typewriter at school, the word processor keyboard did not contain mechanical parts. The typewriter was sensitive to touch and demanded a lot of coordination to use, which ultimately slowed me down. But in the office, I worked much faster.

In 2000, I took a career break and travelled around the world. During that time, I reflected on what I wanted to do next and decided I would like to work with young people who might be experiencing similar difficulties to those I had experienced when I was a teenager. In 2004, I was successful in applying for a position in the learning support department at a local further education (FE) college.

About seven years later, I undertook an undergraduate degree in education and lifelong learning alongside work at the college. The requirement to use a computer to produce essays, rather than handwrite them, was liberating. Studying was more enjoyable. I graduated with first-class honours. The contrast between this and my achievements at school 30 or so years before could not be starker.

Although the teaching on my undergraduate course could have been much more inclusive, the use of an iPad and a proofreader (funded by a Disabled Students' Allowance) made a considerable difference and helped me succeed. Possibly of even greater value were the strategies and approaches I developed to become a resilient and effective learner, drawing on the work of Clarke and Nicholson (2010), Duckworth (2011) and Dweck (2012). Their theories about learning helped me reframe my disabilities in a more objective, positive light. Empowering myself to overcome further challenges and obstacles began with developing knowledge of self and understanding that I had the responsibility and the agency to strengthen my mindset as far as I was able.

After graduation, I became involved in projects advocating the use of technology in teaching and learning, and promoting the importance of good-quality learning support in FE settings. I have spoken at conferences and written for practitioner publications on these topics. In 2016, some of the difficulties I faced as a child with writing reoccurred themselves in the workplace, and as a result, I left FE. The perseverance I needed to survive the school system in the 1970s, and which I developed further through my undergraduate learning, has served me well. It has fuelled a self-belief that makes me feel I can achieve anything I put my mind to. Perhaps this explains, at least in some way, how I got to where I am currently.

For over 40 years, I have had a passion for music, and I have been involved with reggae since the late 1970s. So, after leaving FE, I decided to pursue a dream of setting up my own vinyl record label. At the time of writing, I am a record producer with my own label, managing projects in London, Bristol, Swindon, the USA and Jamaica.

Would I be the person I am today had I taken that ambulance to special school every day? Being a child with SEND educated in a mainstream school had highs and lows. I experienced the acute frustration of trying to learn in a system that was not designed for learners with needs like mine, alongside the fulfilment that came from noticing the lasting strength I gained from successfully overcoming challenge after challenge.

One day, I will return to FE in a role that will allow me to expand on what I have learned about applying the power of mindset to learning and succeeding in the face of adversity. Building resilience and grit, and cultivating a growth mindset are as important as any reasonable adjustment required to successfully include young people with physical difficulties or learning difficulties in mainstream settings.

Forty years ago, the Warnock Report recommended that there should be more opportunities for people with disabilities to become teachers and to work in schools and colleges. The greater visibility of people like me in mainstream settings not only normalises disability but also adds value in terms of providing students with SEND relatable role models.

References

Clarke, J. and Nicholson, J. (2010) *Resilience: Bounce back from whatever life throws at you.* Surrey: Crimson.

Duckworth, A. (2011) *Grit: The power of passion and perseverance.* London: Penguin Random House.

Dweck, C. (2012) *Mindset: How you can fulfil your full potential.* London: Constable and Robinson Ltd.

4 Recognising paradigm shifts

Lessons from the Warnock Report

Klaus Wedell

One of the main strengths of the Warnock Committee's work was that it recognised the advances in the principles and practices for special educational needs (SEN) provision, which had accumulated in the previous ten or more years. The committee's final report, published in 1978, articulated the nature of these advances in an authoritative way that was sufficient to shape the ensuing legislation. So, the Warnock Report provides lessons not only through its achievement but also in showing what it takes to implement change.

In this short chapter, I will first outline the developments in thinking about SEN prior to the Warnock Enquiry, and then consider some lessons about how the committee's formulations were incorporated in subsequent legislation. In the final section, I will consider the question 'where do we go next?'

Developments prior to the Warnock Enquiry

The changes in principles and practice of SEN in the years that led up to the Warnock Enquiry amounted to a 'paradigm shift'. This term, promoted by Thomas Kuhn (1962), has been used in a variety of contexts to explain a profound change in a model or perception of events. Children (I include young people in this definition) we now describe as having SEN used to be described as being 'handicapped by disabilities of body or mind'. These were the words Margaret Thatcher, the then secretary of state for education and science, used in the Warnock Enquiry's terms of reference.

The term 'special educational needs' had already been introduced by Professor Ronald Gulliford in the title of his 1971 book. He was the first professor of special education in the UK, at the University of Birmingham (from 1975 to 1986), and was later co-opted to the Warnock Committee. Use of the term 'special educational needs' amounted to a 'paradigm shift' in people's conceptualisation, from a 'within-child' model of the causation of children's needs, to an 'interactive' one. This emphasised that 'needs' result from causes in children's environment, impinging during their development as well as from causes within themselves. Previously, children were categorised largely in terms of assumed medical causes, which were thought to determine their entire subsequent development. This view assumed that more severely 'handicapped' children could not benefit from the prevailing education system and so were deemed 'ineducable' and excluded from it.

Increasingly, those working and researching in the field both in the UK and in the USA during the 1950s and 1960s were beginning to discover that child-rearing practices and educational approaches could be designed to match children's needs and so to have a compensatory impact for their further development. This interactive, causal view of child development implied that, at any one point in time, children's SEN would occur on a continuum of degrees of severity. The parents of these children came together to fund new educational provisions to improve the outcomes. For example, in the UK, the charitable body which later became the Spastics Society (and in the mid-1990s, Scope) was formed in 1952 to set up special schools for children with cerebral palsy. The parent groups and specialist professionals formed a powerful lobby (Peter, 1996). Their campaigning led to the 1970 Education Act, requiring local education authorities to take responsibility for the education of 'ineducable' children.

During the late 1960s and early 1970s, mainstream schools began to make available a whole system of differentiated provision. This came in the form of special classes and units for children with moderate or more circumscribed difficulties; for example, those with literacy difficulties and those with partial hearing loss. One of the aims of this provision was, of course, the effective inclusion of these children. This change resulted from the orientation of the professionals involved in serving this population, such as educational psychologists (Wedell, 1970). In 1975, the government responded with Circular 2/75 (DES, 1975), which established that there should be an explicit input of educational advice from teachers, head teachers and educational psychologists in the assessment of a child's SEN.

Implications for legislation on SEN

This account offers a brief summary of the background to the Warnock Committee's deliberations and recommendations. These resonated with the prevailing perceptions about SEN and provide a lesson about why the committee's report was effective in exerting pressure on the government to formulate the 1981 Education Act along these lines. However, Sir Keith Joseph, Mrs Thatcher's secretary of state for education and science (1981–1986), rightly recognised that effective legislation would require additional funding. Therefore, he delayed implementation until 1983, when a drop in the school population offered him some financial leeway.

Few would have expected, however, that the 1981 Act would incorporate the interactive view of SEN so explicitly. 'Special educational provision' is defined as relative to the extent to which the general education system is *incapable* of meeting an individual child's needs: 'provision which is [has to be] *additional* to or otherwise *different* from, the educational provision made generally for children of his age in schools' (Education Act 1981). A child's SEN is defined by the extent to which he has a 'significantly greater difficulty in learning than the majority of children of his age', or if 'he has a disability which either prevents or hinders him from making use of educational facilities of a kind generally provided in schools'. The relativity of these formulations, while strictly following the interactive view, leaves open the criteria for assessing the severity of an individual child's needs (Wedell, 2017).

The Warnock Report formulates the likely proportions of children with SEN with reference to epidemiological studies of children in various forms of provision at the time: 'up to one in five children at some time in their school career will require some form of special educational provision' (Section 3.17). Our research on the implementation of the 1981 Act (Goacher *et al.*, 1988), for instance, found that the proportions of children with SEN differed between local authorities and rural and urban areas. Primary legislation, such as an Act of Parliament, has to be supplemented by secondary legislation specifying practical 'guidance' about how provisions made in statute should be implemented. The Department of Education charged the Institute of Education, University of London, to carry out a short research project to find out how the assessment arrangements introduced in Circular 2/75 were working out (Wedell *et al.*, 1982). Following this, the government then issued Circular 1/83 (DES, 1983), which focussed on children with SEN who were in mainstream or specialist provision, as well as on the assessment of those with more severe needs. Circular 1/83 was the predecessor to three successive 'Codes of Practice', created in 1994, 2001 and 2015. Each Code offered guidance on how the Act from which it was derived should be implemented.

Overall, the Codes attempted to deal with the same challenges of identifying and meeting children's needs but each in relation to the particular features of the education system at the time. The most recent Code was formulated in the context of the financial stringency resulting from austerity policies. Consequently, its aspirations have been hard to implement. A separate area of legislation introduced an additional rights dimension to provision for SEN. The government issued non-statutory guidance (DfE, 2014) regarding children who fall within the definition of 'disability' contained in Equality Act 2010. Section 4.2 sets out an obligation to 'treat a disabled person more favourably than a person who is not disabled... as far as is reasonably possible'. Significantly, this explicitly implies positive discrimination.

Where do we go next?

What are the lessons from the Warnock Report? This chapter has attempted to explain how thinking about SEN amounted to a paradigm shift because it recognised the interactive nature of the causation of myriad difficulties and needs children have with learning. The 'special-ness' of SEN was defined in relation to the scope within the education system for a flexible response to an individual's needs. Although there have been remarkable instances of the flexibility with which individual schools respond to children's SEN, the education system as a whole has remained within the nineteenth-century 'factory' model. Teaching and learning take place via grouping children in classrooms, each under the direction of a teacher. Little has changed, for example, in reconceptualising the role of the teacher in the information technology age. It is hardly surprising that the 1981 Act's conditions for inclusion still persist: that educating a child with SEN in an 'ordinary' (mainstream) school 'is compatible with: his receiving the special educational provision that he requires; the provision of efficient education for the children with whom he will be educated; the efficient use of resources' (Section 2(3)).

Attempts to extend ways to meet individual children's SENs have amounted to little more than 'patching up' the limitations of the prevailing system (Wedell, 2008). A Commission on Education, funded by the Hamlyn Foundation, was set up in 1991 as the result of wide concern about the education system in general and how it might develop in the subsequent 25 years. The Commission published a set of papers in 1993. In my paper on special education (Wedell, 1993), I wrote:

> It would seem incredible that looking back from 2018 that we had not been using the organisational and pedagogical flexibility that existed already in 1993 to respond to the demands of the broad and balanced curriculum and pupils' learning needs.

Nowadays, the potential for 'flexibility' in relation to time and place for learning has already advanced through all the opportunities offered by digital technology. The education workforce includes a wider range of areas and degrees of further professional specialisation; for example, among SEN coordinators and the more targeted participation and contribution of teaching assistants (Webster *et al.*, 2016). We aspire towards better cross-disciplinary collaboration between professionals in education, health and social services. In particular, we now have a greater recognition that children with SEN and their parents and carers are partners in education. And still we have not fully faced the 'dilemmas and tensions inherent in inclusive education' (Norwich and Koutsouris, 2017) nor grasped that the conceptualisation of an education system has to fundamentally start from acknowledging that all children are different.

Such a conceptualisation could amount to a paradigm shift from the present situation. But how could it come about? The Warnock Committee recommended that a government-funded Special Education Research Group (SERG) should be established to 'provide a synoptic view of what is going on and offer guidance on priorities' (Section 18.11), but this proposal was not followed up. However, in 1982, the Voluntary Council for Handicapped Children (VCHC), which predated the Warnock Enquiry, persuaded the government to fund a working party to explore the possible role and function of the Warnock Report's recommendation for a National Advisory Committee. The working party, of which I was a member, was chaired by George Cooke, the vice-chair of the Warnock Committee. Although its brief was mainly focussed on service coordination at a national level, its recommendations also included the aspiration that a national advisory committee would 'look ahead... discern the emergence of new demands and develop new ideas and practices' (VCHC, 1984). Unfortunately, the government at that time turned down the working party's recommendations.

So, to conclude on the second question posed in the title of this book, would it be wise to follow the Warnock Committee's lesson about the need for a SERG? At a time of concern about the state of the current education system – for example, that it is fragmented (Bernardes *et al.*, 2015) and that schools are facing difficulties in responding to children's needs (House of Commons, 2018) – instituting a SERG could offer a crucial strategy for recognising the urgency of a paradigm shift in thinking about an education system to match children's SEN.

References

Bernardes, E., Shaw, B., Menzies, L. and Baars, S. (2015) *Joining the dots: Have recent reforms worked for those with SEND?* London: Driver Youth Trust/LKMCo. Available online: https://driveryouthtrust.com/wp-content/uploads/2016/08/DYT_JoinTheDotsReportOctober2015.pdf. Accessed on: 6 August 2018.

Department for Education (DfE) (2014) *The Equality Act 2010 and schools.* London: DfE. Available online: www.legislation.gov.uk/ukpga/2010/15/contents/enacted. Accessed on: 6 August 2018.

Department for Education and Science (DES) (1983) *Assessments and statements of special educational needs (Circular 1/83).* London: DES.

Department for Education and Science (DES) (1975) *The discovery of children requiring special education and the assessment of their needs (Circular 2/75).* London: DES.

Education Act 1981, c.1. Available online: www.legislation.gov.uk/ukpga/1981/60/section/1/enacted. Accessed on: 6 August 2018.

Education (Handicapped Children) Act 1970. Available online: www.legislation.gov.uk/ukpga/1970/52/contents/enacted. Accessed on: 6 August 2018.

Goacher, B., Evans, J., Welton, J. and Wedell, K. (1988) *Policy and provision for special educational needs: Implementing the 1981 Education Act.* London: Cassell Educational Ltd.

Gulliford, R. (1971) *Special educational needs.* London: Routledge and Kegan Paul.

House of Commons Education Committee (2018) *Forgotten children: Alternative provision and the scandal of ever increasing exclusions. Fifth report of session 2017–19.* London: House of Commons. Available online: https://publications.parliament.uk/pa/cm201719/cmselect/cmeduc/342/342.pdf. Accessed on: 6 August 2018.

Kuhn, T. (1962) *The structure of scientific revolutions.* London: University of Chicago Press.

Norwich, B. and Koutsouris, G. (2017) 'Addressing dilemmas and tensions in inclusive education', *Oxford Research Encyclopaedia of Education.* Oxford: Oxford University Press. Available online: http://education.oxfordre.com/view/10.1093/acrefore/9780190264093.001.0001/acrefore-9780190264093-e-154. Accessed on: 6 August 2018.

Peter, M. (1996) 'Lobbying for special education', in I. Lunt and B. Norwich (eds.) *Psychology and special educational needs.* Aldershot: Arena.

Voluntary Council for Handicapped Children (VCHC) (1984) *A national advisory committee for special educational needs?* London: VCHC.

Webster, R., Russell, A. and Blatchford, P. (2016) *Maximising the impact of teaching assistants: Guidance for school leaders and teachers.* 2nd ed. Oxon: Routledge.

Wedell, K. (1970) 'Diagnosing learning difficulties: A sequential strategy', *Journal of Learning Difficulties*, 3(6), pp. 23–29.

Wedell, K. (1993) 'Special education: The next 25 years', in *Briefings for the National Commission on Education*. London: Heinemann.

Wedell, K. (2008) 'Confusion about inclusion: Patching up or system change?', *British Journal of Special Education*, 35(1), pp. 127–135.

Wedell, K. (2017) 'SENCos coping with the relative definition of special educational needs', *British Journal of Special Education*, 44(2), pp. 220–222.

Wedell, K., Welton, J. and Vorhaus, G. (1982) 'Challenges in the 1981 Act', *British Journal of Special Education*, 9(2), pp. 6–8.

5 Including children and young people with complex needs in learning and life

Peter Imray

How far have we come since the Warnock Enquiry?

There can be no doubt that much has been achieved since the Warnock Enquiry reported the extensive findings, which informed and shaped the 1981 Education Act. But educational inclusion is not one of them.

At the time of writing, the proportion of children in full-time education with low incidence, highly complex needs is rising (Pinney, 2017; DfE, 2018), putting more and more pressure on an already stretched mainstream sector. This is, however, not a temporary, isolated or peculiarly English phenomenon but a trend indicating that the philosophy of inclusive education, as a process of increasing participation and decreasing exclusion from the culture, community and curricula of mainstream schools (Booth *et al.*, 2000), is in deep crisis.

Roger Slee (2018) reasonably highlights the relationship between democracy and inclusion, urging us to 'not walk away from democracy and inclusion', as 'both are worth fighting for'. Yet arguing for inclusion for some is as difficult as arguing for democracy for some, even if that 'some' are the vast majority. On this point at least, Slee and I are at one; educational inclusion as a philosophy is meaningless unless we pursue it for all.

Slee argues that full inclusion has been achieved 'in schools and communities whose commitment to inclusive education for all comers has been successful'. Really? How can this be when it is not possible for a proportion of the school population to succeed within the common curriculum? Over the 30 years since its introduction in 1988, *not one single pupil* with either severe learning difficulties (SLD) or profound and multiple learning disabilities (PMLD) has ever succeeded beyond, *at the very best*, the very earliest stages of England's statutory National Curriculum. The vast majority have not even made it to the start, even by the time they leave school at 19. If making it to the start of a curriculum after 14 years of full-time education is the summit of our ambition, this is inordinately poor ambition. At worst, this should represent a national disgrace, and at the very least, surely this indicates that it is the wrong curriculum.

Importantly, this persistent failure has nothing to do with the quality of the teaching or the type of school in which children and young people with SLD or PMLD have been educated. Neither is it attributable to the resources applied to the school or the degree of differentiation. It is a definitional issue. If those with SLD and PMLD could succeed within a curriculum designed for typically developing pupils, they would not have SLD or PMLD (Imray and Colley, 2017). This is because the developmental beginnings of the National Curriculum are beyond the developmental endings of these groups of learners, and the degree of their learning difficulties are too complex for them to catch up within an academic, linear curriculum model (Imray and Hinchcliffe, 2014). Such difficulties are simply not open to the level of amelioration necessary for academic success. These learners 'are forgotten. They don't just fail a little. They fail a lot, and their noses are rubbed in their failures' (Kauffman, 2002).

Some critics have suggested that the curriculum can be rewritten, or even redesigned, so that all learners are included from the start, as in Universal Design for Learning (see, for example, Hall *et al.*, 2012; Rose *et al.*, 2014), or the inclusive pedagogy of Florian and Black-Hawkins (2011). Both of these positions assume, however, that such redesigning has not occurred, or at least has been half-hearted. In the UK – and I strongly suspect in every other country attempting to achieve educational inclusion nirvana – this really is not true. All special schools, which currently educate 46 per cent of pupils with Education, Health and Care Plans (DfE, 2018), have, over the last 30 years, adapted, rewritten, differentiated, altered and redesigned the National Curriculum ad nauseum. Yet pupils with complex special educational needs and disabilities (SEND) still fail to reach the start. To continue to pursue a philosophy that does not, and indeed cannot, work is to continue to fail a small but significant group of learners year after year after year. This cannot be acceptable.

There are an increasing number of inclusionists who sit on what Norwich (2013) terms the 'moderate' wing, and, whilst accepting that there are problems with regard to the universal view that 'all means all', nonetheless continue to support the philosophy of inclusion, despite the definitional problems. Hornby (2015) makes a valiant attempt and certainly argues strongly against the workability of a universalist view but ends up describing the current English education system as a model for 'inclusive special education'. I believe that he has a point when he says that, in practice, the broad mix of mainstream and special school options work well, but does it describe educational inclusion? Perhaps we should turn full circle and go back to Mary Warnock's argument, put forward in her much-publicised rethinking on the issue. Rather than being concerned with 'all children under one roof', we should be much more concerned with including all children in the 'common goal of education' (Warnock, 2005).

Such a stance brings to mind Nussbaum's (2007) contention that a theory – in this case, inclusive education – may be admirable, yet have 'serious limitations in some area or areas'. Shuttleworth (2013) points out that practitioners and policymakers often have 'exclusion clauses' pinned to their inclusion arguments. Hansen (2012) goes so far as to suggest that the 'conceptual identification' of inclusion needs to establish that 'exclusion processes are an internal part of inclusion processes'.

Within this framework it seems reasonable to ask two key questions. First, is educational inclusion possible if some must be excluded for who are these 'some', and why should they alone be excluded? And second, how can we support an alternative watered-down philosophy that has no workable and agreed definition?

Where do we go next?

In a very interesting analysis of the reasons why we educate young adults with SLD, Black and Lawson (2017) took a critical look at the Studio, part of the provision for young adults at Greenside School in Hertfordshire, England, an all-through (2–19) special school for pupils with severe and complex learning difficulties. Their analysis of educational paths, functions and purposes of learning identified three main purposes of education for all learners: person-becoming, later life/vocation and citizenship. Black and Lawson (2017) suggest that:

> [For] learners with SLD, and as demonstrated through the Studio evaluation project, we have noted that: (1) these purposes of education are particularly difficult to disentangle; and (2) vocational learning is afforded a much wider interpretation as preparation for adult life and independence more generally, with preparation for employment as relevant to only some learners.

That is, in the UK, our ambition for adults with SLD is much reduced from the rest of the population, with their chances of employment of any description almost nil. Imray and Colley (2017) put it thus:

> In the UK at least, we seem to have accepted the 'inability' of those with SLD and PMLD to work, yet this should be intolerable to any civilised society. We believe that the enormous good will within the academic community towards those with disabilities could be more usefully garnered to fighting for real social inclusion, rather than almost exclusively fighting for educational inclusion.

In an attempt to overcome this obvious problem, Equals, a UK charity working with and for children, young people and adults with SLD and PMLD, have recently developed a semi-formal SLD curriculum (Equals, 2017). This is perhaps the first of its kind in the world. The curriculum seeks to address the fact that children with SLD do not and cannot succeed within a conventional 'inclusive' curriculum. Equals concur with Black and Lawson's thoughts on curriculum development for those with complex learning needs, as well as earlier writings, such as that of Dee, Devecchi and Florian (2006) and their 'being, having, doing' pedagogy. But Equals argue strongly that a curriculum emphasis on person-becoming, later life/vocation and citizenship must start *much* earlier than 16 years (and at least as early as eight or nine years) if all are to maximise their potential.

This view echoes Amartya Sen's and Martha Nussbaum's Capabilities Approach (Sen, 2005; Nussbaum, 2011), which states that society must seek to maximise all learners' opportunities to be the best they can be and do the best they can do, irrespective of their disabilities. Johnson and Walmsley's (2010) key analysis of 'a good life' for people with learning difficulties supports the adoption of a Capabilities Approach that encourages a reimagining of social contracts and a reshaping of social roles and structures in order to create a truly inclusive democracy.

The point being, of course, that inclusion, and the spirit of inclusion, is not just about education. There really is no point to educational inclusion if it merely reinforces social exclusion. Those who fail at school will have a higher chance of failing after school, and we do not need a phalanx of research articles to tell us that this must be so.

Educational inclusion has a problem: it does not work for all children. As Albert Einstein so eloquently put it, we cannot solve our problems without changing our thinking. To continue to pursue a 'least restrictive environment' policy, to campaign for more children in mainstream and fewer in special schools, on a point of unworkable principle, ignores the facts and may merely promote what Hodkinson (2012) calls 'inclusion as spectacle'. Children with complex needs learn differently. If they learn differently, we ought to be teaching them differently and teaching them different things. That is *different*, not differentiated, since a common curriculum, however differentiated, will not work.

Further and equally as damning, such a policy continues with the wholly unreasonable expectation that all teachers can be specialists for all children, no matter how complex the learning difficulty. This just does not make sense. We do not expect it of lawyers or doctors or even car mechanics; why are we expecting it of teachers?

We need to begin again, from a position of ensuring that *all* agencies are set up to ensure that *all* children can maximise their opportunities to be the best they can be and do the best they can do – whatever that is and wherever and however that can be best attempted. We are a long, long way away from that. It may not be achievable, but at least it is possible, and that is, perhaps, a good start.

References

Black, A. and Lawson, H. (2017) 'Purposes of education for young people with severe learning difficulties: Exploring a vocational teaching resource – 'A stepping stone to...' what?' *Cambridge Journal of Education*, 47(2), pp. 207–226.

Booth, T., Ainscow, M., Black-Hawkins, K., Vaughan, M. and Shaw, L. (2000) *The index for inclusion: Developing learning and participation in schools.* Bristol: Centre for Studies on Inclusive Education.

Dee, L., Devecchi, C. and Florian, L. (2006) *Being, having and doing: Theories of learning and adults with learning difficulties. LSRC research report.* London: Learning and Skills Network. Available online: http://files.eric.ed.gov/fulltext/ED508507.pdf. Accessed on: 26 July 2018.

Department for Education (2018) *Special educational needs in England: January 2018.* Available online: www.gov.uk/government/statistics/special-educational-needs-in-england-january-2018. Accessed on: 13 August 2018.

Equals (2017) *Equals Semi-Formal (SLD) Curriculum.* Newcastle: Equals. Available online: www.equals.co.uk. Accessed on: 26 July 2018.

Florian, L. and Black-Hawkins, K. (2011) 'Exploring inclusive pedagogy', *British Educational Research Journal*, 37(5), pp. 813–828.

Hall, T.E., Meyer, A. and Rose, D.H. (2012) 'An introduction to Universal Design for Learning: Questions and answers', in T.E. Hall, A. Meyer and D.H. Rose (eds.) *Universal design for learning in the classroom: Practical applications.* New York: Guildford Press.

Hansen, J.H. (2012) 'Limits to inclusion', *International Journal of Inclusive Education*, 16(1), pp. 89–98.

Hodkinson, A. (2012) 'Illusionary inclusion: What went wrong with New Labour's landmark educational policy?' *British Journal of Special Education*, 39(1), pp. 4–10.

Hornby, G. (2015) 'Inclusive special education: Development of a new theory for the education of children with special educational needs and disabilities', *British Journal of Special Education*, 42(3), pp. 234–256.

Imray, P. and Colley, A. (2017) *Inclusion is dead: Long live inclusion*. London: Routledge.

Imray, P. and Hinchcliffe, V. (2014) *Curricula for teaching children and young people with severe or profound learning difficulties*. London: Routledge.

Johnson, K. and Walmsley, J. (2010) *People with intellectual disabilities: Towards a good life?* Bristol: The Policy Press.

Kauffman, J.M. (2002) *Education deform: Bright people sometimes say stupid things about education*. Laham, MD: Scarecrow Press.

Norwich, B. (2013) *Addressing tensions and dilemmas in inclusive education*. London: Routledge.

Nussbaum, M.C. (2007) *Frontiers of justice: Disability, nationality, species membership*. Cambridge, MA: Harvard University Press.

Nussbaum, M.C. (2011) *Creating capabilities: The human development approach*. Cambridge, MA: Belknap Press.

Pinney, A. (2017) *Understanding the needs of disabled children with complex needs or life-limiting conditions*. London: Council for Disabled Children/ True Colours Trust.

Rose, D.H., Meyer, A. and Hitchcock, C. (eds.) (2005) *The universally designed classroom: Accessible curriculum and digital technologies*. Cambridge, MA: Harvard University Press.

Sen, A. (2005) 'Human rights and capabilities', *Journal of Human Development*, 6(2), pp. 151–166.

Shuttleworth, M.A. (2013) 'Inclusion is…. Musing and conversations about the meaning of inclusion', in A. Azzopardi (ed.) *Youth: Responding to lives*. Dordecht, The Netherlands: Sense Publishers.

Slee, R. (2018) *Inclusive education isn't dead, it just smells funny*. London: Routledge.

Warnock, M. (2005) 'Special educational needs: A new look', in L. Terzi (ed.) *Special educational needs*. London: Continuum.

6 Pre-service teacher training and special educational needs in England, 1978–2018

Looking back and moving forward?

Dr Alan Hodkinson

In the 1970s, higher education institutions (HEIs) began to introduce optional special educational needs elements into their initial teacher training (ITT) programmes. Problematically, the variable quality and availability of such courses meant that newly qualified teachers (NQTs) often felt ill-prepared to teach children with special educational needs and disabilities (SEND). The Warnock Report recognised that a lack of training acted as a barrier to the integration of pupils into mainstream education.

In her report, Warnock concluded that increasing the knowledge base of teachers was of the 'upmost importance'. The committee's recommendations advocated that teachers should be able to recognise the early signs of SEND and that training teachers should develop knowledge of segregated education and specialist advisory services. The report further stated that student teachers should understand: developmental difficulties (such as physical, sensory, emotional, behavioural or learning); the steps necessary for meeting a child's needs; the attitudes needed for dealing with SEN; and, how to modify classrooms and the curriculum.

Interestingly, Warnock believed it was not appropriate for training teachers to engage in the in-depth study of disabilities and that teachers should not have to provide children with specialist help themselves. She was, though, under no illusion as to the immensity of the task ahead. As Section 12.12 of the Warnock Report states:

> Some 40 years will need to elapse from the time that the proposed special education element is introduced before it can be assumed that all teachers have undertaken such an element in the course of their initial training.

ITT and SEN in the 1980s and early 1990s: a postcode lottery of provision?

The Warnock Committee's recommendations relating to teacher training were incorporated into Circular 3/84 (DES, 1984). This specified criteria that student teachers needed to achieve to attain qualified teacher status (QTS). Additionally, the training of students in aspects of hearing impairment or severe learning difficulties were now phased out of most ITT programmes (Jones, 2006). During this period, the government shifted the focus of the provision of SEND into the realms of in-service training and continuing professional development courses.

ITT came under scrutiny again with the advent of a state curriculum for schools in 1988. HEIs were told to include SEND issues within their programmes but were not offered advice as to how they might achieve this. The lack of a steer from government meant that ITT grew organically through the late 1980s and 1990s, with the quality of training subject to a postcode lottery. In 1990, Her Majesty's Inspectorate (HMI, 1990) concluded that the provision of SEND in ITT was, in the main, inadequately preparing new teachers for their future employment. Despite such criticism, many HEIs continued using established methodologies. In reality, SEND tended to have a Cinderella status within ITT programmes (Thomas, 1993). Garner (1996) concluded that this period witnessed growing uncertainty within HEIs as to what SEND training should include and how it should be delivered.

New Labour: the metrification of ITT

From 1997, New Labour began a period of reform that progressively increased the prescription and control of ITT (McNamara *et al.*, 2008). For example, in documents entitled *Excellence for All* and *Programme of Action*, New Labour specified that student teachers should gain more practical experience of working with children with SEND (Vickerman, 2007). Interestingly, some two decades after the Warnock Report, government once again correlated successful inclusion with teacher training. However, despite this intervention, there was, in reality, little change to how student teachers were trained in SEND in many HEIs.

In 1998, a radical restructure of ITT saw the Teacher Training Agency (TTA) take control of pre-service training. Henceforth, all trainees, as they were now designated, needed to meet a set of standards to gain QTS (Golder *et al.*, 2005). However, the standards were not welcomed by HEIs (Barber and Turner, 2007), with many of them believing they were an 'official script emphasising the discipline and control of children' rather than support for children with complex disabilities (Allan, 2003). Whilst government had specified what should be taught, it again failed to prescribe how SEND training should be organised and delivered. During this period, then, the government failed to heed the warnings of the past, continuing to minimise the coverage and influence of SEND within ITT.

Training in the twenty-first century

The century began with further reductions in the time allocated to SEND, as focus within ITT turned to the National Strategies for numeracy and literacy. In 2002, the TTA introduced yet another set of standards for QTS. Just 3 out of the 42 standards related to SEND. This iteration conceptualised training in SEND in terms of minimalistic, technical standards of compliance. Commenting on these standards, Basingstoke (2008) noted that the government's lack of action had enveloped its policy within a 'groundhog day'. Ofsted (2003), reiterating Warnock's critique, stated that teachers 'were being asked to lead children with significant learning needs... without enough learning'. In 2004, the government again confirmed its commitment to including children with SEND in mainstream classrooms, stating that it would work with the TTA and HEIs to ensure that ITT 'provide[s] a good grounding in core skills and knowledge of SEN' (DfES, 2004).

In addition, in the same year, government made clear its expectation that every teacher had to be a teacher of children with SEND and that they should be equipped with the 'skills to do so effectively' (Lambe, 2007). Somewhat like a scratched record, then, once again, the government was promoting training as the panacea to all ills but did little to provide forward momentum on these issues. In reality, while 'much [had] changed in our classrooms' (Winter, 2006), 'little had really changed in the ways trainees were prepared in relation to SEND' (Moran, 2007).

SEND training: moving forward?

In 2007, the successor of the TTA, the Teacher Development Agency (TDA) responded to issues raised with respect to the inclusion road map (DfES, 2004) predictably enough, by calling for improvements in trainees' knowledge and skills, through which they could be helped to deliver a more inclusive learning experience for pupils. Unusually, though, on this occasion, something new did actually happen. The TDA initiated a project in some HEIs, focussing on SEND training modules. Despite positive responses from trainees' and HEIs' to these modules, there was no official record of the number of trainees who had received this training. Basingstoke (2008) suggested, therefore, that in reality nothing had changed, and he urged the government to ensure that SEND training became a compulsory part of all ITT programmes.

In 2007, yet another set of new standards were introduced. Again, 3 standards (out of a total of 33) related to SEND. The government believed these were an important vehicle for the development of trainees' knowledge of SEND. These standards, though, were again criticised for promoting a 'technicist approach' of auditable competencies (Pearson, 2007). Evidence from the NQT survey from that year (TDA, 2007) suggested that although there was a small increase in trainees' preparedness to teach children with SEND, some 48 per cent still felt unprepared. Other research (e.g. Moran, 2007; Ofsted, 2003) was more pessimistic, indicating that 89 per cent of trainees felt that they did not have the confidence to teach children with SEND and that some HEIs were providing training that was judged only 'adequate'.

Subsequent official reviews of SEND during this period (e.g. Lamb, 2009; Salt, 2010) added to the evidence of the variable quality of ITT programmes (Lawson *et al.*, 2013). In response, in 2012, the TDA published training materials to be used in HEIs. However, despite this, just a few years later, the DfE-appointed Carter Review of ITT (DfE, 2015) still found significant gaps in SEND training. Indeed, it concluded that there was an urgent need to improve pre-service training in this area.

Again, as in 2007 and 2012, the government seemingly responded in a purposeful manner to a critique of ITT. HEIs must now ensure that trainees understand the SEND Code of Practice, and in addition, they have to equip trainees with strategies to ensure that they can access the National Curriculum and that all pupils might make progress within this curriculum. This stipulation reflects the element of the current Teachers' Standards (DfE, 2011), which requires trainees to know how to adapt teaching to respond to the strengths and needs of all pupils.

Conclusions

The history of ITT, as evidenced earlier, shows that despite government rhetoric and purposeful intervention, little has actually changed in relation to SEND training since the Warnock Report of 1978. So, 40 years after its publication, we again stand at a crossroads looking back but trying to move forward in relation to teacher training.

The jury is, though, still out in relation to whether current government interventions will pay dividends in relation to the quality and consistency of training programmes. The history of ITT suggests that we cannot assume that the latest government initiative will be successful. What we do know, however, is that Warnock's assessment of the immensity of the task of training teachers is as true now as it was in 1978.

References

Allan, J. (2003) 'Productive pedagogies and the challenges of inclusion', *British Journal of Special Education*, 30(4), pp. 175–181.

Barber, N. and Turner, M. (2007) 'Even while they teach, newly-qualified teachers learn', *British Journal of Special Education*, 34(1), pp. 33–39.

Basingstoke, M. (2008) *Hansard* – Col. 589–600.

Department for Education (DfE) (2015) *Carter review of initial teacher training*. London: DfE.

Department for Education (DfE) (2011) *Teachers' standards: Guidance for school leaders, school staff and governing bodies*. London: DfE.

Department for Education and Skills (DfES) (2004) *Removing barriers to achievement: The government's strategy for SEN*. Nottingham: DfES.

Department of Education and Science (DES) (1984) *Initial teacher training: Approval of courses (Circular 3/84)*. London: DES.

Garner, P. (1996) 'A special education? The experiences of newly qualified teachers during initial teacher training', *British Educational Research Journal*, 22(2), pp. 155–165.

Golder, G., Norwich, B. and Bayliss, P. (2005) 'Preparing teachers to teach pupils with special educational needs in more inclusive schools: Evaluating a PGCE development', *British Journal of Special Education*, 32(2), pp. 92–99.

Her Majesty's Inspectorate (HMI) (1990) *Special educational needs in initial teacher training*. London: HMI.

Jones, G. (2006) 'Department for Education and Skills/Department of Health Good Practice Guidance on the education of children with autistic spectrum disorder'. *Child Care Health and Development*, 32, pp. 543–552.

Lamb, B. (2009) *The Lamb Inquiry. Special educational needs and parental confidence*. Nottingham: Department of Children, Schools and Families.

Lambe, J. (2007) 'Student teachers, special educational needs and inclusion education: Reviewing the potential for problem-based e-learning pedagogy to student practice', *Journal of Education for Teaching*, 33(3), pp. 259–377.

Lawson, H. Norwich, B. and Nash, T. (2013) 'What trainees in England learn about teaching pupils with special educational needs/disabilities in their school-based work: The contribution of planned activities in one-year initial training courses', *European Journal of Special Needs Education*, 28(2), pp. 136–155.

McNamara, O., Webb, R. and Brundrett, M. (2008) *Primary teachers: Initial teacher education, continuing professional development and school leadership development*. Primary Review – Research briefings. Cambridge: Primary Review/University of Cambridge.

Moran, A. (2007) 'Embracing inclusive teacher education', *European Journal of Teacher Education*, 30(2), pp. 119–134.

Ofsted (2003) *Special educational needs in the mainstream*. London: Ofsted.

Pearson, S. (2007) 'Exploring inclusive education: Early steps for prospective secondary school teachers', *British Journal of Special Education*, 34(1), pp. 25–32.

Salt, T. (2010) *Independent review of teacher supply for pupils with severe, profound and multiple learning difficulties (SLD and PMLD)*. Nottingham: Department of Children, Schools and Families.

Teacher Development Agency (TDA) (2007) *The newly qualified teachers survey 2007*. London: TDA.

Thomas, D. (1993) 'Gritty, sensible and utilitarian – the only model? Special educational needs, initial teacher training and professional development', in A. Dyson and C. Gains (eds.) *Rethinking special needs in mainstream schools*. London: David Fulton.

Vickerman, P. (2007) 'Training physical education teachers to include children with special educational needs: Perspectives from physical education initial teacher training providers', *European Physical Education Review*, 13(3), pp. 385–407.

Winter, E.C. (2006) 'Preparing new teachers for inclusive schools and classrooms', *Support for Learning*, 21(2), pp. 85–91.

7   The rights of the child with special educational needs

Dr Maggie Atkinson

The education and well-being of children with special educational needs and/or disabilities (SEN/D) are subject to debates in which passions run high on all sides. Giving them chances to succeed features in parenting, policymaking, practical guidance and statutory direction, as well as in media coverage of 'worst cases'.

These debates surface both within and beyond education. Professionals in education, social care and health inevitably approach the issues from different positions. Families, however, want all these differing professions and professionals to see their children as people, as individuals, not as a constellation of contested difficulties and diagnoses. That it is complex to do this well is not denied. Recognition that it is the professionals concerned – not the families of these children – who should make the complexity navigable is urgently required.

Children with SEN/D and their families are experts by experience. They deserve a leading stake in ensuring outcomes. Legislation since 1981 has sought to highlight the needs of these children, with the most recent legislation, introduced in 2014, seeking to engender a rights-based approach by developing local offers, undertaking earlier intervention and the creation of Education, Health and Care Plans (EHCPs) to be developed and delivered collaboratively by all agencies. EHCPs replaced Statements of SEN, introduced via the 1981 Education Act. Neither of these statutory documents has fully lived up to the promise of providing extra help, increasing children and families' stake in the process, and reducing the bureaucratic burden and stress of statutory assessments and review.

This chapter considers progress towards the promotion and protection of rights for children with SEN/D under the United Nations Convention on the Rights of the Child (UNCRC) (1989). The UNCRC is an international human rights treaty. It was adopted and opened for signature in November 1989, and came into force in September 1990. Having ratified it in 1991, the UK is bound by it. The UN defines children as those under 18 years old, though in some jurisdictions these rights are retained beyond that age. In England, for those with SEN/D, it extends to age 25. The same right is extended to care leavers; a group where the incidence of SEN/D is above average.

The core principles of the UNCRC are: non-discrimination, so rights apply to all (Articles 1 and 2); action in the best interests of the child (Article 3); life, survival and development (Article 6); and respect for views of the child, sought in accordance with age and stage of development, then listened to and acted on (Article 12). Rights in the Convention are inviolable and cannot be ignored. Adults – all of us – are, therefore, duty bearers.

UNCRC Article 23 relates to special needs and/or disabilities. Paraphrased, it says that a mentally or physically disabled child should enjoy a full decent life in conditions ensuring dignity, promoting self-reliance and active participation. States Parties recognise their rights to special care, and shall encourage and ensure the extension, subject to available resources, of assistance appropriate to the child's condition and the circumstances of parents/carers. Assistance shall be free whenever possible and designed to ensure that the child accesses and receives education, training, healthcare, rehabilitation, preparation for employment and recreation opportunities in a manner conducive to achieving the fullest possible social integration and individual development.

Article 24 relates to physical and mental health services, enabling children to access all other rights. They are active partners, helping to shape services which respond to their inputs. Like some other articles, Article 24 has a 'general comment' that exemplifies what life is like when the right is fulfilled. Articles 28 and 29 relate to education. All children, without exception, have a right to education that develops their abilities, aptitudes, attitudes, tolerance and awareness of the wider world.

Are we there yet?

Much energy is invested in trying to get the system to deliver what the UNCRC affirms as rights for all children. In England, delivering them across education, health and social care has been made more challenging by shrinking resources since at least 2010. Our most vulnerable, disadvantaged children, young people and families have been hardest hit by reductions in essential, now chronically underfunded, services. This is exacerbated by fragmentation in publicly funded schooling and the sometimes despairing, sometimes wilful, behaviours of a minority of schools towards children who do not 'fit the box' for whatever reasons: for example, in the recent emergence of the phenomenon of off-rolling.

All those trying to fulfil the rights of the child face dwindling budgets; embattled families; and, in the worst cases, service-specific resistance to change, despite clear requirements in legislation. Since the enactment of the Children and Families Act 2014 in England, Ofsted and the Care Quality Commission have conducted joint inspections of local SEN/D planning, provision and partnerships. Whilst they have found good practice, in too many localities they report disjointedness and poor delivery of the Act's ambitious change programme (Ofsted/ CQC, 2017). In particular, the voice of the child in shaping what happens is patchily heard, and its expression ill-supported (Office of the Children's Commissioner, 2014).

On this evidence, and much more that a chapter this brief cannot cover, assurance of the rights of children and young people with SEN/D, enshrined in laws underpinning the practical implementation of Acts of Parliament, remains out of pace with what the UNCRC asks of us all. The UN Committee regularly reminds the UK that it is not fully delivering the UNCRC. Making better progress towards doing so remains the object of ardent and necessary campaigning by advocates, charities and the Children's Commissioners in each UK nation.

The bottom line is that, as a vulnerable child, the likelihood your rights will be denied rises with every vulnerability. If you cannot defend your rights, and adults cannot or will not ensure them, the claims you make as a rights holder are denied. If you are last to be included in what your peers do, at school or anywhere else, or actively excluded, the system has questions to answer, and much work to do.

Children are not waiting to be adults to claim these rights. They already have them. It is our responsibility to ensure they are fulfilled.

References

Office of the Children's Commissioner (2014) *"They still need to listen more": A report about disabled children and young people's rights in England*. London: Office of the Children's Commissioner. Available online: http://dera.ioe. ac.uk/21631/1/They_still_need_to_listen_more_a_report_about_disabled_ childrens_rights_in_England.pdf. Accessed on: 9 August 2018.

Ofsted/Care Quality Commission (CQC) (2017) *Local area SEND inspections: One year on.* London: Ofsted/CQC. Available online: www.gov.uk/government/ publications/local-area-send-inspections-one-year-on. Accessed on: 9 August 2018.

The United Nations (1989) *The United Nations convention on the rights of the child*. Available online: www.cypcs.org.uk/rights/uncrc/full-uncrc. Accessed on: 9 August 2018.

8 'Equality, belonging, value, humanity'

Tara Flood

Four decades ago, the idea that disabled children and young people[1] could be included in mainstream education was radical. Now, 40 years on from the Warnock Enquiry, we are at a crossroads – or possibly a cliff edge. Either way, the reality is that much of the good intentions and aspirations for inclusion have been dismantled by a Government whose ideology for education is about elitism, competition and academic results. It is an ideology that runs counter to the Government's own commitment to building the capacity of mainstream education to be more inclusive of disabled pupils, as set out in the UN Convention on the Rights of Persons with Disabilities (2018).

Forty years ago, I, like so many disabled children, was institutionalised in a residential special school. I spent the vast majority of my childhood there, separated from my family and community, whilst the system attempted to normalise me. Thankfully, they did not succeed!

So, has Baroness Warnock's vision been successful? I think to a degree, it has, insofar as that many more disabled children and young people are educated in mainstream settings than there would have been if it had not been for the work of the Warnock Committee. But is it *really* inclusion? Again, for some, the answer is yes. But the practice and policy changes coming out of Warnock saw disabled pupils as the 'problem' to be fixed or normalised. And little has changed today.

A book revisiting Mary Warnock's oft-described U-turn on inclusion in 2005 was published in the run-up to the 2010 general election (Warnock and Norwich, 2010). In it, Warnock described how many disabled pupils were being let down by a 'one size fits all' education system: schools lacking resources; teachers feeling under enormous pressure to deliver impossible and unrealistic targets to ensure their school achieves a high ranking in the league tables; parents facing increasing struggles to find places for their children in local schools; children and young people having their creativity restricted by an inflexible and unimaginative curriculum; and assessment and accreditation systems that take a deficit approach to disability. All these barriers still exist today, some 14 years on, but they are a great deal worse when you throw the effects of austerity into the mix.

The Warnock Report failed to grasp the difference between 'integration' and 'inclusive' education. Integration is where disabled pupils, including those with special educational needs (SEN), are placed in mainstream education with some adaptations and resources but on the condition that they can fit in with pre-existing structures, attitudes and a largely unaltered environment. This reflects the experience of many disabled pupils today. Warnock described and promoted 'integration', not inclusion in the sense that we at the Alliance for Inclusive Education (ALLFIE) understand it. With real inclusion, disabled pupils are placed in mainstream provision where there is a commitment to removing all barriers to full participation. And each and every child – disabled and non-disabled – is a valued, unique individual.

Inclusion can and does work. It takes a whole system approach that recognises the human right of every pupil, whatever their learning difference, to be part of, and well supported in, a single education system. Such a system will not happen overnight because it requires extensive planning; new thinking; and, ultimately, the political will to deliver change.

However, much as it pains me to say it, the current education system in the UK does not allow for the real inclusion for *all* disabled pupils because there are systemic barriers that prevent, deny and exclude them. Also, there are no incentives to develop inclusive practices. That said, there are many schools up and down the country who fully include a wide range of disabled children and young people with all the labels of complex, profound and multiple needs. For example: Eastlea Community School in Newham; Emersons Green Primary School in Bristol; and Blatchington Mill School and Sixth Form College in Brighton.

In England, we have a principle of 'presumption for mainstream' enshrined in law. It is better to have it than not, but it does not deliver inclusion. It is essentially about getting through the door of an education setting, but it says little about what goes on once a child or young person is through that door. The reasonable adjustments duty in the 2010 Equality Act is often quoted as the solution to the failings of the legal principle, but it is not sufficient. It relies so much on what is determined to be 'reasonable' at any given time. In the age of austerity, what is and is not 'reasonable' can often be determined by what is and is not affordable.

Even with the 'presumption for mainstream' principle and Government rhetoric about parental choice, we have an education system that, for some disabled children and young people, is inherently bias towards segregated provision. Parental choice is only a reality if parents accept what they are offered. If parents challenge a local authority or education provider, they are almost certainly facing a difficult, lengthy and expensive legal battle to get redress.

Government rhetoric also talks about children getting a good education. But what does that mean? Good for whom – or what? Essentially, children that can learn in a standardised way have greater value because they are more likely to enhance a school's academic performance indicators by producing good SATs and GCSE results. Those children that cannot contribute in this way, because testing and assessment regimes are not accessible, are increasingly seen as surplus to requirements. The education system in England is anything but child-focussed. Children have become the fuel that stokes the furnace of competition between schools. I do not blame schools. I blame a Government that refuses to see the real value in every child.

There is the evidence to support the claim about the redundancy of some children and young people within our education system; and some of the most indicting evidence is collected by Government itself. Disabled children and young people are disproportionately represented in annual school exclusion statistics (DfE, 2018). Meanwhile, official census data show the number of disabled pupils in mainstream settings has been declining year-on-year since 2010 (ALLFIE, 2017).

Last summer, the United Nation's Disability Committee scrutinised the UK's implementation of the UN Convention on the Rights of Persons with Disabilities (UNCRPD). It concluded that the Government's approach to disabled people is causing a 'human catastrophe' (Disability Rights UK, 2017). Certainly, the telephone calls ALLFIE receive from parents every day supports this view. The UN Committee set out a number of recommendations that, if implemented, would deliver a truly inclusive education system, placing the rights and needs of all pupils and students at the centre.

Despite the doom and gloom, I believe there are glimmers of hope. There are the schools that are bucking the trend and parents who gather together locally to challenge and oppose cuts to local SEN support services – and with a degree of success (Ward, 2018). And we have some direction from the UN Disability Committee on how our system can improve.

The UNCRPD is at the heart of everything that ALLFIE believes in. Taking Article 24 – the right to an inclusive education – as our starting point, we need now to build real aspiration for all our children and young people. We need to move away from sticking with what has become familiar: a tradition of practice and policy that sees disabled children and young people as 'the problem'. There are vested interests in keeping it that way and factors around accountability that prompt school leaders to make the wrong decisions – all of which we need to resist.

We need to celebrate good inclusive practice in mainstream settings and share it. We need to look and learn from other education systems: for example, Finland, where a belief in the value of all children has not damaged their ranking in international performance tables. Why? Because they value academic and vocational learning equally, and they value all learners too; the Finnish system is not segregated. Similarly, many areas of Canada have not had special schools for decades. The UK needs to take a deep breath and do the same.

What happens when schools are inclusive and welcome in disabled pupils? Perhaps the final word should come from someone who has direct experience of the struggle and the success: the parent of a disabled young man who made the transition from a mainstream primary school to mainstream secondary school.

> The term 'inclusion' gets talked about a lot, especially when a box needs to be ticked. Inclusion for me means so much more than that. It means equality, belonging, value, humanity. My son has all sorts of labels that mean he needs additional support to learn. He is not going to be able to access GCSEs, and so we are struggling to find a mainstream school that will accept him. My son is not going to be an academic high achiever, but he needs and deserves a good education. He also needs and has a right to be part of the world, have friends and feel part of his community. We want him to be part of mainstream world, not separated out because he can't perform well in tests. To me, inclusion is about everyone, and it benefits everyone. Do we really need to compartmentalise children by their ability to take tests? Inclusive education is about there being no excuses for not including any child – disabled or non-disabled. Accept this fact and work it out.

Note

1 At the Alliance for Inclusive Education, we include pupils with SEN in our definition of disabled children and young people because we consider the SEN labelling process disablising because it is based on a deficit model of disability.

References

Alliance for Inclusive Education (2017) *10% decline of disabled pupils with SEN attending mainstream schools is a shocking indictment of the Government's lack of commitment to human rights. General Election press release.* Available online: www.allfie.org.uk/news/press-releases/10-decline-of-disabled-pupils-with-sen-attending-mainstream-schools/. Accessed on: 13 August 2018.

Department for Education (2018) *Permanent and fixed-period exclusions in England: 2016 to 2017.* Available online: www.gov.uk/government/statistics/permanent-and-fixed-period-exclusions-in-england-2016-to-2017. Accessed on: 13 August 2018.

Disability Rights UK (2017) *A human catastrophe – New UN condemnation for UK human rights record.* Available online: www.disabilityrightsuk.org/news/2017/august/human-catastrophe---new-un-condemnation-uk-human-rights-record. Accessed on: 13 August 2018.

United Nations (2018) *Convention on the rights of persons with disabilities.* Available online: www.un.org/development/desa/disabilities/convention-on-the-rights-of-persons-with-disabilities.html. Accessed on: 13 August 2018.

Ward, H. (2018) Legal win 'will encourage more challenges to SEND cuts', *Tes.* Available online: www.tes.com/news/legal-win-will-encourage-more-challenges-send-cuts. Accessed on: 13 August 2018.

Warnock, M. and Norwich, B. (2010) *Special educational needs: A new look.* London: Continuum.

9   The chapter that nearly didn't get written

Nancy Gedge and Sally Phillips

NANCY: This is the story of what happens to relatively sane people when they have to deal with the Education, Health and Care Plan (EHCP) process. As mothers of boys with Down's syndrome, we have dealt with the three powers of education, health and social care since the moment of their birth. Knowing many other parents who are in the same position, we have a story to tell: of love, of loss and, frankly, of frustration.

SALLY: It's a wonder this chapter got written. What were we doing, saying yes? My to-do list is as long as my leg – and I have small writing: get private speech and language therapy; chase NHS speech and language therapy; get private occupational therapy; chase NHS occupational therapist; find counsellor; chase special school counsellor; fill in personal independence payment form; write new parent's report for new ECHP; meet other parent whose child has just been excluded from nearby school; submit evidence to government SEND review, find out why Olly's always so tired, what that rash is... I could go on. We are our children's therapists, teachers and legal aid. And if we're not doing it for our own kids, we're doing it for others.

NANCY: Because I'm a teacher, maybe I thought I'd have plenty of time in the long summer holiday to write, in between the catching up with all the things I didn't get done before the end of term: the hospital visits I put off because they were in the middle of term, and the endless sorting out that is my lot, now that my son, Sam, has left what I now realise are the comforting arms of the school, and entered the unfamiliar world of post-16.

SALLY: Putting families at the centre of the EHCP process sounds great, but admin is not my strong suit. I'm not a lawyer, and as I said, my to-do list is the length of *War and Peace*. I cannot manage. I can't do it and I'm not alone. The endless meetings, checking and report writing is overwhelming.

NANCY: I have gone back and forth to the LA. I sent the draft EHCP back at least three times. I found out about case law and quoted it in snippy letters I didn't want to write. I used up my precious free time. Friends have fallen by the wayside as I have struggled to keep on top of it all. What should be somebody else's job has fallen to me. I may as well have written his EHCP myself, from beginning to end. Apart from anything else, when your child has a condition like Down's syndrome, which comes along with communication difficulties, it can make finding out what they want an art in itself. One year he told me he wanted to be an Eddie Stobart lorry. Another year, in his Annual Review, he said simply, and rather movingly, he wanted to be a man. Some children may refuse to answer such questions. Others, especially those on the autism spectrum, will try to tell you what they think you want to hear; a different answer for each different, well-meaning professional.

SALLY: I wrote ten emails to the local authority with no reply. I eventually went in and chased someone around the desk to get an answer. It's not just parents; SENCOs are drowning in paperwork too.

NANCY: I conducted a survey of SENCOs for *Tes* (Gedge, 2018). I found that some SENCOs, especially those in primary schools, are trying to fit the role in to a Friday afternoon. How can it be that, instead of being the person who supports teachers to teach children like ours effectively, SENCOs are left struggling under an admin load, coordinating the whole operation with no clerical support? The reality is that the role of the SENCO is hugely variable. Much of it is misunderstood, much of it is under-resourced and much of it is under-respected.

SALLY: It's four years since the Children and Families Act 2014 was introduced. All statements were supposed to have been converted to EHCPs by March 2018, yet some remain unwritten (Keer, 2018). Official statistics show that the demand for special schools is on the up. To add insult to injury, parents are asked to input to government consultations to suggest how we resolve these issues. That is if any of us get time, after we have come back from tribunal, had three visits to the paediatrician, and found a podiatrist.

NANCY: How did parents end up being the ones to hold local authorities and schools to account for the provision they're supposed to put in place for our children? Is it not Ofsted's job to check everyone was doing what they were supposed to be doing, and getting on with educating our young people in an equitable way? All children in a classroom have different needs. Responding to individuals and helping them move their learning on is what teachers do – regardless of whether they have SEND.

SALLY: In the UK, we seem to be moving away from inclusion and building more and more walls. Instead of helping everyone improve, the system tries to move everyone closer towards the mean. Since when were we in Britain trying to be average? It does not need to be like this. In the 1980s, Italy closed special schools. As of 2011, 99.99 per cent all school-aged children with disabilities in Italy were educated in inclusive general education classes (Anastasiou *et al.*, 2015). I think they just shut them all one summer and reopened in September with everyone in mainstream. Obviously, that was chaotic, but it got it done. Inclusive education is a human rights issue. It is non-negotiable. Calling them 'special needs' doesn't help. These are human needs. There is evidence that if classrooms and teachers adapted to children with SEND, no one loses out – and in fact, everyone might do better (Hehir *et al.*, 2016; Szumski *et al.*, 2017).

NANCY: I cannot help thinking, that against all the calls for more funding to support learners with SEND – which I know we desperately need – without a change of heart, nothing much will be different. Throwing money at the system, without looking at the influence and impact of accountability measures, league tables, the long-standing attitudes that we encounter far too often in local authorities and schools, and lack of attention SEND has in teacher training and ongoing professional development, is not – and is never going to be – the answer. SEND is a complicated area. It demands a nuanced response.

SALLY: I would choose attitude over funding any day. For instance, at my son's primary school, there was an expectation that Olly would be included. In the first sports day, everyone cheered for him. At the last one, hardly anyone noticed. He was just one of the class, and that's how it should be. Expectations were high. The staff and other pupils expected him to participate and to say things that might be worth listening to. They didn't patiently wait for him to finish when he started speaking.

NANCY: It's time to put to death the idea of difference and competition in education, because after all, we all have the same rights to it. Making provision for disabled children – no matter what the disability – is not an added extra. It is, or it should be, what we do every day. Every time we call it 'inclusion' – or integration or special or whatever – we make out that what we're doing for those with disabilities is different to what we're doing for everyone else. It's time for change, and this time, for the better. Instead of blaming individuals, we need to look at – and I mean honestly look at – the constraints pushed on all of us – parents, teachers, school leaders, SEND officers and caseworkers in local authorities – by the mixed-up, confused system within which we work.

SALLY: We need to make it more attractive for schools to want our kids. Olly's wonderful learning support assistant at primary school gave the football team that included Olly a goal head start, so everyone wanted him in their team. Why not give schools incentives? We teach children about society, and school is where and how we do it. If we know our neighbours, we think of them as human beings, and so many of the things I fear most for Olly stem from society thinking of him as slightly less than human.

References

Anastasiou, D., Kauffman, J.M. and Di Nuovo, S. (2015) 'Inclusive education in Italy: Description and reflections on full inclusion', *European Journal of Special Needs Education*, 30(4), pp. 429–443. Available online: www.researchgate. net/publication/279961505_Inclusive_education_in_Italy_description_and_ reflections_on_full_inclusion. Accessed on: 13 September 2018.

Gedge, N. (2018) Undermined, underused and misunderstood: Life in schools for Sendcos. *Tes*, 13 February. Available online: www.tes.com/ news/undermined-underused-and-misunderstood-life-schools-sendcos. Accessed on: 13 September 2018.

Keer, M. (2018) *Zombie statements: Councils to miss legal EHCP transfer deadline for thousands of children*. Available online: https://specialneedsjungle. com/zombie-statements-councils-miss-legal-ehcp-deadline/. Accessed on: 13 September 2018.

Hehir, T., Grindal, T., Freeman, B., Lamoreau, R., Borquaye, Y. and Burke, S. (2016) *A summary of the evidence on inclusive education*. Sao Paulo: Instituto Alana. Available online: https://alana.org.br/wp-content/uploads/ 2016/12/A_Summary_of_the_evidence_on_inclusive_education.pdf. Accessed on: 14 September 2018.

Szumski, G., Smogorzewska, J. and Karwowski, M. (2017) 'Academic achievement of students without special educational needs in inclusive classrooms: A meta-analysis', *Educational Research Review*, 21, pp. 33–54.

10 Normalising difference

Resetting perceptions of SEND in the media

Jon Severs

I can admit now that I was afraid of Adam. He wandered up, smiled and asked me my name. And I froze, momentarily, because this conversational, social 15-year-old in the school reception room was not acting how I had been taught autistic people would act. I had prepared myself for something different. I was nervous because that difference scared me. Meeting Adam shamed me, for he made it clear that I had bought into a myth and then recycled it, propagated it and adjusted my own actions to fit within it.

Adam was not the last pupil in a special school to make me feel this way. Meeting him was not some miracle cure for the misconceptions about special educational needs and disabilities (SEND) that I held. Rather, every single time I meet a child with SEND, I reset my expectations and my 'knowledge'. And every time I have the privilege of talking with some of the excellent teachers in the specialist sector, the same thing happens.

I was not a novice in SEND before joining *Tes* – my brother-in-law has very complex learning difficulties; several friends teach in the specialist sector – but I was certainly ignorant. And now, six years on and still being challenged every day, I ruminate often about why our starting point with SEND is so negative. How even someone relatively informed like me can buy into a narrative so baseless.

It comes, I have concluded, from a process of 'othering' those with SEND. We do this as a society, not always consciously but certainly conspicuously. Think hard about presentations of people with SEND in the media, in film, even in conversations with friends. So often we talk about the diagnosis, not the person. So often we rely on cardboard cut-outs of that diagnosis. And so often we fall into what I might call 'permitted' feelings towards those with SEND.

The first of these feelings is pity. It seems we are comfortable with SEND if pity is our reason for engagement. Whether it be the television programme *The UnDateables*, the mainstream primary school inviting children from the local special school to their sports day or applauding an autistic person's 'special talent' (so problematic in itself), the power relationship is clear: we are looking *at* them, doing things *for* them, seeing our involvement with them as an act of charity. We box them into a space that is safe for us, but in doing so, we rob them of their agency.

Another way we engage is through a feeling of curiosity. So often, the person with SEND becomes their diagnosis, and the diagnosis becomes the basis for the whole interaction. We want to explore how 'it' makes them feel, what 'it' makes them do, what causes 'it'. We attribute everything to the diagnosis. The person becomes an exhibit. We tie them down to that diagnosis and do not let them escape it because exploring beyond it scares us and requires us to engage differently.

And finally, there is obligation: we feel we should do something, so we do enough to make us feel better, and then we tuck them away until we next feel like we need to prove we are 'OK' with disability.

The media has to take some responsibility for this. In film, television and journalism, we are guilty of portraying people with SEND in ways that invite pity and curiosity. Occasionally, coverage of SEND is an obligation; a segment or an article is needed to 'make up the numbers'. If someone with SEND is part of a story, the SEND becomes key to that story, and it is brought to the fore. It is reductive, inaccurate, irresponsible and inexcusable.

We also silence narratives. That power balance is alive and well in the media's limited and perpetual representations of SEND. We do not give equal weight to the narrative of a person with SEND. We position it, again, as charity, curiosity, obligation.

Our expectation of what inclusion was supposed to achieve has not helped. Perhaps there is a version of inclusion that is less about *every* child being educated in a mainstream school and centred more on *every* child seeing *every* other child equally. In a dynamic where inclusion rests on the proviso that those with additional needs conform to educational and social norms in (and beyond) school, how much room is there to celebrate diversity?

Too often, I would say, difference is problematised. Talk to enough parents of children with SEND, and you begin to build a picture of the 'othering' that takes place: 'This school is not right for your child', 'This type of learning is not right for your child', 'Your child would be better off in a small group working with a teaching assistant'.

Underneath it all, lies this: 'Your child is different, and we do not know what to do with difference'. And that – whether we like it or not, whether we notice or not – is what us adults model to children. That and fear. Because so often, marginalisation is not done through malice but through a fear of difference and of our own helplessness.

So, how do we begin to fix this? Exposure is the first step. We need to find ways to give everyone the kinds of experiences I have had at *Tes* and, crucially, to do so in ways that do not invoke pity, obligation or curiosity. We in the media can share examples of schools that accept or celebrate difference and to do so authentically – not in ways that appear tokenistic.

We try to do this on *Tes*. Encouragingly, I see SEND becoming more visible in the mainstream media through programming and articles. Increasingly, we are hearing not just about people with SEND but *from* people with SEND: their issues, their views and their achievements – not their diagnoses.

It is about a process of demystification and assent to difference, too: we accept deviations in behaviour which are not labelled with a diagnosis as being in the 'normal' range, but give someone a diagnosis and we suddenly deem them to be on another scale altogether. Changing that is about learning from the excellent practice of the many special schools who work so hard to move away from labels and labelling, who do not let challenges become excuses, who are acutely aware of the effects of learned helplessness.

It is about seeing the whole of humanity as being on a spectrum, not just those with autism, and responding to individual differences in all of us, not just those that have a medical certificate. And most of all it is about seeing these kids, like Adam, for who and what they are, and accepting that, taking away pity and curiosity and obligation and fear. True inclusion is an acceptance of difference rather than an obsession with it.

11 The debate continues...

Vijita Patel

The schools sector is locked in deep debates about the inclusivity of education. Breakdowns within the system manifest polarised viewpoints and drive the conversation between pragmatics and ideology. The dialogue often gravitates to the distinction between integration and inclusion. This highlights a tension relating to whether children and young people with and without special educational needs (SEN) could and should be educated within the same school, instead of within or across a range of settings, which would include the specialist settings that complement mainstream.

The legacy of Warnock Report, and the paradigm shift it defined, is evident in how these issues are framed. In replacing 'educationally subnormal' with 'special educational needs', it established the educability of students with additional needs as a fundamental premise. The legislation that followed responded and gave momentum to a change in perceptions that ensured children with additional needs with SEN were visible and legally protected. The taken-for-granted premise on which our discussions about the education of children and young people with SEN are based – upholding every child's right to education and school leaders' collective responsibility for the population as a whole – is palpable evidence of the Warnock Enquiry's impact.

The shift towards 'special educational needs' was intended to move understanding from a medical model to a social model. Instead of labels of deficit, our discourse is now more marked and defined by a discourse of provision for diverse needs. Without a doubt, continued debate is needed to challenge shortcomings and to hold our systems and actions to account. This is particularly critical in times of rapid change. The need to keep discussion near the surface can be related to the pressures on families and schools seeking to navigate a constantly moving system, which is itself responding to an increase in the population of students with needs and a challenging financial landscape.

There is a crucial conduit between mainstream and specialist schools, which mobilises the dialogue, exploration and context for truly inclusive pedagogy and curriculum design. Approaches to teaching, learning, engagement and personal development without compromising the holistic needs of SEN profiles is a focus for those working in specialist and mainstream settings and is reflected in professional learning partnerships. The relationship between the two ensures the needs of the child are at the heart of provision design and promotes social inclusion through partnership. Through a shift in values, schools are recognising the need to prioritise and promote meaningful inclusion; to shape and define what quality first teaching means and looks like for a wide spectrum of needs.

The binary choice implied in the debate about whether a child's education ought to be delivered purely in a mainstream school or in a specialist setting is reductionist and overlooks the diversity of schools and the range of expertise that sits within them. It is through collaboration, not simple choice, that the needs of the SEN population are best met locally. Structures within the school-led system, such as teaching schools, give visibility to the strengths and unique characteristics of individual schools, and promote connectivity at the local and national level.

Teacher education and initial teacher training programmes blend pedagogical approaches from mainstream and specialist settings. To see trainee teachers having the majority of their school-based training in special schools, with placements in mainstream schools, is one of the greatest signs of progress. So too is the opportunity for trainees in mainstream primary and secondary schools to receive part of their school-based training in a special school. Both models deepen trainee teachers' engagement with inclusive pedagogies because one size does not fit all.

Would we have special schools leading alliances of mainstream primary and secondary schools without the Warnock Report? The potential in specialist and mainstream settings sits not in isolation but in dialogue and shared evolution. Our best resource is not static but fluid; it is in how we shape and develop our workforce and our environment, and how we aid our young people to move between and through our school system in readiness for life beyond it. There is a solid foundation from which we are building, and further collaboration between schools and employers – to recognise every young person's potential and right to contribute to society, with purpose, through what they 'can do' – will advance this further. The shift in mindset and values that precipitated this journey owes much to the Warnock Enquiry.

12 Swimming against the tide

Vic Goddard

Education is a fundamental right for *every* young person in the UK. There is nothing controversial about that statement, surely? However, if you read responses on social media to just about any article, research piece or blog on the topic of inclusion, you will see that some people find such a remark contestable. It does seem that in the 40 years since the publication of Baroness Warnock's report, some things have changed a great deal, but some remain painfully stubborn.

To be clear, being 'inclusive' does not mean putting the needs of one young person above the needs of every other child in the class. Being inclusive does not mean allowing violence, aggression or rudeness to anyone in the school community. Being inclusive is not about dropping standards to the lowest common denominator. Similarly, having a young person with special educational needs and disabilities (SEND) in a school does not mean that they are going to be naughty or rude. This is one of my biggest gripes when I see any sort of Twitter spat about this issue: there is a presumption that SEND and challenging behaviour go hand in hand.

This obvious nonsense is frequently used in overly simplified arguments by those who then build on their skewed perception with a personal or hearsay example of being 'abused' by a young person with an Education, Health and Care Plan (EHCP). Staff should not be abused by any young person, and making poor behaviour choices is, of course, not limited to young people with SEND. It is a gross piece of prejudice to assume such a link where none exists: it is amazing the way that such 'profiling' can be accepted as fair and balanced comments in lazy minds.

Perceptions of inclusion

More than 1 in 20 young people at my mainstream secondary school has an EHCP, and we have many, many more students with recognised additional needs. I asked some of my students about their perception of inclusion. The message that came back was quite clear: for almost all of them, inclusion was not really something they tend to think or talk about. But do not mistake this for indifference. In much the same way as fish do not notice water, Passmores students see inclusion as a part of the culture. It is not about choice. As one student put it, 'Why would we exclude anyone from our school for things they have no control over?'

There were comments from students about how they got frustrated sometimes when their learning was interrupted by the poor behaviour of one or two individuals. But tellingly, they did not make a mental leap from this to saying that those students should not be in our school. They just wanted this kind of behaviour 'dealt' with quickly. This is the response I would have hoped for. Overall, our students see being part of an inclusive society (in this case, our school, as a microcosm of society) as just how things should be.

That our students think about inclusion this way says a lot about the staff at Passmores. When I asked the staff about inclusion, they expressed a real sense of pride in the inclusive approach we take. They spoke of 'service' and 'community', of inclusion being the right thing to do for everyone. Staff were honest, too, and said that it made their jobs a bit more challenging at times; meeting the needs of a diverse school population takes more planning time.

There was also a feeling that it was *necessary* to be inclusive, given the alternative perspective some other schools have about inclusion. These are the schools that prefer 'the right sort of pupil'; the ones that tell parents that their child with SEND would be better off at the 'school down the road'. I hear this again and again in my meetings with other head teachers. If a school like that has not popped into your mind in the last few moments, consider this: it could be *your* school that everyone else is talking about!

I asked my amazing SEND Coordinator, Angela – a passionate and committed advocate for all young people, and especially those she works with directly – whether the Warnock Report achieved what it set out to do. Her view is illuminating:

> Warnock stated that she never intended that all children, no matter the severity of their needs, be included within a mainstream system of education. I have had admission requests from children who are so severe that special schools refuse to admit them. However, a mainstream school admission is enforced, because legally we are required to meet all needs. Worse, sometimes the need for specialist education is recognised, but the special schools are full.

We are now stuck in a legally-enforced admissions system when the wellbeing of the child is completely ignored. Warnock later called the inclusion of children with severe needs in mainstream education 'extremist'. Local authorities and, occasionally, parents have been empowered to enforce inappropriate admissions. The casualty in this is the child. I love our inclusive community, but being inclusive is too often being used to cover shortfalls in specialist provision and to hide the severe underfunding for these vulnerable young people. As an advocate, I will continue to do all I can to support all young people, but I must also challenge others when they are making decisions for the wrong reasons.

System failure?

For years, government after government has underestimated the need to provide the funding to fully realise the recommendation of the Warnock Report, the legislation that followed in the 1981 Education Act and the SEND Codes of Practice (1994, 2001 and 2014). SEND is persistently overlooked in policy terms. For example, in 2016, the then secretary of state for education, Nicky Morgan, produced a white paper, *Education Excellence Everywhere*, which did not contain a single mention of students with additional needs.

I am fearful that the inclusion agenda has been used as a way to make it look as if governments are meeting the needs of this vulnerable portion of society, without actually taking responsibility. The reality is that schools have been amazing at doing just enough to get by; our skill in sticking plasters over things and carrying on is something to be proud about – but it is also part of the problem. Is 'doing enough to get by' good enough for our children? The tension in the system regarding funding has reached a critical point. Local authorities are struggling for spaces in special schools and they do not have enough money to fund and service the statutory assessment requests they receive. Sadly, the teachers and school leaders among us could name students that have failed in our settings because we did not get the funding support we both needed and requested.

Being inclusive means swimming against the tide. As I have written elsewhere, inclusion is fundamentally about 'botheredness' and resources (2016). And yet educating students with an EHCP is a financial punishment for schools. It is understandable, then, why some schools are not as inclusively minded as we would like them to be. Compared to a school without any students with EHCPs, my school was over

£370,000 'worse off' in the last school year (2017/2018). Money is so tight, and this is a killer for inclusion. Herding students with SEND into high and low concentrations across a town or local authority area makes a mockery of the term inclusion. By its very nature, inclusion means being accepted wherever you are; it should not be conditional or available via a long commute.

If we truly want a system that works for every child in the community, it will take fundamental changes to the regulation of the education system, through Ofsted and, probably more significantly in the world of academies, through the Regional School Commissioners. I think it is a universally accepted truth that having a fully inclusive intake provides a different set of challenges. This is further compounded by the rapid changes in assessment regimes. I was reassured, then, when I heard the then National Schools Commissioner, Sir David Carter, recognising that some communities will take longer to improve results as they are already 'playing catch up'. The rest of the system needs to acknowledge that meaningful inclusion does not happen in a vacuum and is made more or less achievable by what is happening in wider contexts.

The Warnock Report did much to improve the prospects of many young people with SEND in trying to access and contribute to society through education. It emphatically tackled much of the offensive labelling of children and young people with disabilities. For our students at Passmores, inclusion is unremarkable; something that barely draws comment. To them, why would a school be anything other than inclusive? However, we still have a way to go before the same can be said of our comprehensive education system. Thinking and acting inclusively should be a school's default setting, but it will take a shift at central government level to make it happen.

Famously, it is how a society treats its weakest members that is the true mark of a civilisation. The Warnock Report signalled the direction of travel. The journey continues.

Reference

Goddard, V. (2016) *The problem with inclusion.* Available online: https://pass morespedagogy.wordpress.com/2016/11/18/the-problem-with-inclusion/. Accessed on: 25 September 2018.

13 Special educational needs and the power of the arts

Andria Zafirakou

Editor's note

Members of the Warnock Committee conducted many school visits as part of their enquiry. While they reported being impressed with the concern shown for individual pupils with special educational needs and disabilities (SEND), they concluded that the quality of the education offered to them was 'in some respects less satisfactory [and] sometimes limited in scope and challenge' (Section 11.1).

Warnock recognised that an appropriate curriculum for learners with SEND, in both mainstream and specialist settings, was essential for achieving two things. First, it provides a space within which 'good personal relationships' could be fostered between the teacher and the pupil; and second, it provides the kinds of stimuli and opportunities for engagement in learning required for motivating pupils at risk of educational failure. No doubt informed by evidence the British Association of Art Therapists and Arts Research Society gave to the enquiry, Warnock singled out the creative subjects for their particular relational, motivational and therapeutic power:

> Relationships are often developed within well planned educational activities which are recognised by the individual as both serving his needs and being intrinsically interesting. This is particularly true of arts subjects which, if well taught, may be of great benefit in their own right, as well as being media for therapies.
>
> (Section 11.61)

In this chapter, arts and textiles teacher, and winner of the 2018 Global Teacher Prize, Andria Zafirakou explains how a carefully nurtured bond of trust, together with her belief in the transformational potential of the creative arts, helped Joe (not his real name) successfully transition from a specialist setting and thrive in a mainstream school.

Joe's story

I had the absolute privilege of teaching Joe, a young man with a complex SEND profile. By secondary transition, the achievement gap between Joe and his peers had grown so wide that his sense of self and his confidence were shattered. He transferred from the local mainstream school, where he spent his primary years, to a specialist provision. By then, Joe's communication disorder had settled into severe selective mutism. During his time at the special school, Joe felt the benefits of a curriculum that was personalised and built around his needs and strengths. He made significant progress and, most crucially, found the strength to communicate independently. The occasions when Joe retreated to selective mutism were always outside of the special school environment; predominantly in the local community, when the social demands on him escalated.

Joe's mother was desperate for him to be educated in an environment that would address and support his emotional well-being. The professionals working with Joe and his family recognised that he needed a school that could help him regain his confidence, recognise what he could do and support his growth.

Our school had a strong partnership with Joe's special school, supporting cohorts of pupils moving into our mainstream comprehensive at Key Stage 4. Through this partnership, we gained incredible professional development from our special school colleagues, as we promoted the social inclusion of these fantastic young people. It has shaped who are as a school community in the most necessary way.

So, through careful discussions with Joe, his family and both schools, it was agreed that Joe would transfer to Alperton Community School. We knew that the best way to support Joe and to help him realise his potential was by working with a core set of teachers. Together, we would ensure his social interaction priorities led to the further development of his self-confidence and help him overcome the challenges his communication disorder presented in social situations.

We knew the arts were subjects that gave Joe opportunities to shine. In leading the design of Joe's curriculum and timetable, my priority was to ensure we used the creative arts as a vehicle to equip him with the skills that would support his development and his transition into adulthood. Art was the greatest tool in helping build that crucial bond with Joe.

My pedagogical approach prioritises authentic relationships with my pupils. My starting point is to understand who they are and what took them to this point. I use this to develop a bond that allows them to trust me and to share their challenges. Teaching Joe informed my reflections on pedagogy and classroom management in a way that will stay with me forever. That process took time and a range of strategies, which were not always verbal.

Through this process, we got to the heart of Joe's self-awareness, and it helped him to own the things he wanted to strengthen. His confidence boosted his acquisition of skills, and his talents were surfacing with increasing momentum. He was a gifted artist, and by the end of Key Stage 4, he had earned a GCSE grade C in art and finished Key Stage 5 with a grade B in his A-level art exam. Even more powerful was the improvement in his confidence. Within a large, busy mainstream comprehensive school, Joe had forged for himself an identity built on his strengths and talents.

As a Global Teacher Prize winner, I have had the pleasure and privilege to work with teachers across the world. In many countries, Joe's story could have been very different. He could have remained mute. His education could have been limited. His changing needs might not have been recognised. His mother's wish for changes to his provision may not have been acted on, let alone voiced. His potential unrealised.

The impact and legacy of the Warnock Report means that none of this was Joe's fate. In the UK, teachers face all kinds of challenges and barriers, but our approach means that pupils like Joe can, and do, have their needs recognised and met, and schools and families can work in partnership to unlock their talents.

14 Moving special education on
Teaching, conversation and love

Ruth Cigman

To most truly teach, one must converse; to truly converse is to teach.

Tharp and Gallimore (1988)

In the introduction to this book, Rob Webster writes that 'we should not be seeking to emulate or replace the Warnock Report, but to move it on'. I agree. The report has been severely criticised and, like me, Webster finds much of the criticism misplaced. But what is meant by 'move it on'? In this chapter, I shall discuss the report philosophically.

Baroness Warnock is a distinguished philosopher, but in her writings for a wider public, she rarely refers to philosophy directly. I believe that moving the Warnock Report on requires a faculty about which she has written extensively: the imagination. We must think in ways that are not dry but imaginative, not detached but practically and emotionally engaged. This has always been Warnock's aim.

A reasonable metaphor, I think, for Warnock's educational philosophy is that *true teaching* is a kind of solvent through which educability is realised. Salt is soluble, but it will not dissolve without a solvent like water. Educability, similarly, may never be realised in the absence of true – that is, truly excellent – teaching. But what does this mean? How can we *make* good teachers?

In *Cherishing and the good life of learning* (Cigman, 2018), I explore these questions, building on the following passage by philosopher of education, Joseph Dunne (2005):

> The great art for teachers is to be responsive not only to the opportunities and demands of the specific practice but also to the needs, aptitudes and difficulties of particular pupils.

Dunne then quotes Tharp and Gallimore on true teaching and true conversation (as have I at the start of this chapter). True conversation is not necessarily, or exclusively, an exchange of words; it includes gestures, tones, facial expressions, sighs, etc., bearing meanings that may or may not be grasped.

Warnock endorsed my book before publication, approving the idea of true conversation as the 'essence of teaching'. Of course, there are educational challenges with children who cannot see, hear or walk, and good teachers are responsive to these. Extra provision may be needed, but this requirement does not go to the heart of teaching itself. To say that true conversation belongs at the heart of true teaching is to say that *conversational needs* – requiring sensitivity to individual understandings and misunderstandings, or partial understandings – should occupy a central place in education. Such needs may be persistent or rare, profound or mild; every learner is susceptible to them.

In the interview in Chapter 2, Warnock responds to a question about how successfully we train teachers to meet the needs of children by highlighting the relational aspect of teaching: 'My guess is that teacher training doesn't give enough attention to personal relations between teachers and pupils'. One thing, she continues, is essential: teachers should be trained to love, cherish and nurture their pupils. In this way, they will discover 'who's floundering, who is in difficulties, who needs extra help'.

In short, we should not shy away from the idea of love, which is associated with the idea of true conversation. Part of what this means – for Warnock, I believe, as well as myself – is the propensity to attend imaginatively and sympathetically to the meanings an individual seeks to convey. Teacher training – the endeavour to 'make good teachers' – must involve the cultivation of this propensity, or in many cases something more like permission to develop and express it with children.

Many educationists retreat into the comfortable domain of technique. This is not so much wrong as incomplete, as suggested by the 1978 report:

> Close and continuous observation of all children by their teachers is essential... teachers must be equipped to notice signs of special need... They must appreciate the importance of early assessment and know when and where to refer for special help... This knowledge and appreciation should be taught to all teachers in the course of teacher training.
>
> (Section 12.4)

Knowledge may seem easier than appreciation to incorporate into teacher training courses, but without the latter, the former is compromised. Appreciation, involving attention to individuals as described, brings urgency to the quest for robust knowledge.

When the Warnock Report recommended that a 'special education element' be included in all courses of initial teacher training, it affirmed the much discussed continuum between so-called 'special' and 'non-special' needs. The majority of children with special needs, says the report, are likely to 'manifest their difficulties for the first time in school' and 'will have to be identified there' (Section 12.4). The distinctive *telos* for teachers, then – their proper function – is to respond to *all* children in fundamentally the same way. Through 'close and continuous observation' – informed, as Warnock added, by love or cherishing – teachers must be conversationally responsive (in Dunne's words) to the 'needs, aptitudes and difficulties of particular pupils'.

Although the term 'special' is a mark of progress (a clear advance over 'handicapped'), I believe it should be reviewed in the light of a philosophy of love. Potentially if not actually, confusion is generated by the claims, first, that children's individual needs should be the focus of teaching and, second, that a certain proportion will turn out to be 'special' and the rest 'non-special'. The point is not that the statistics are wrong, but that they bring preconceptions. We expect children with autism to have special conversational needs – this expectation is frequently justified – but teachers should be equally alert to 'non-special' children who, on occasion, experience such needs. The idea of a continuum points towards a ragged, rather than statistical, conception of specialness.

Historical influences on Warnock's thinking include Aristotle, Kant and Sartre. Here follows a brief sketch of these influences.

Flourishing

Warnock became concerned about the legacy of the 1978 report when her daughter, a teacher, told her about the reality of many children with autism in mainstream settings: 'They did not flourish, they were miserable and they tended to be bullied. That is what started me off' (McKie, 2005). Many philosophers, including Warnock, see flourishing (*eudaimonia* in Greek) as the basis of a good human life and the primary aim of education. We may think of it as a cross between happiness (or pleasure) in the English sense, reasonable good fortune and learning or human development. The Greeks were not interested in happiness without learning or development, and some good fortune (e.g. true teaching) is needed if this is to come about.

Human dignity

Unlike Aristotle, for whom the flourishing of slaves hardly mattered at all, Kant saw all human beings as fundamentally equal. One must never treat humanity, he said, 'simply as a means, but always at the same time as an end'. This is contravened by the principle that all children must be educated in mainstream schools in order to build an inclusive society, irrespective of the suffering or compromised learning of some. Combining Aristotle with Kant, 'no child is ineducable' means that the flourishing of every child matters equally and incontrovertibly.

Inclusion

Baroness Warnock's reservations about inclusion are well known. Writing in *Tes* in May 2018, she says she was 'delighted' when the former secretary of state for education, Michael Gove, promised to 're-move the bias towards "inclusion"'. I suggest that she meant the bias towards *institutional* inclusion, as distinct from *ethical* inclusion. To retain the Kantian concept of human dignity is not – as Warnock understands very well – to be 'biased' towards inclusion. It is to include every child in the fold of *true teaching*, as required for a flourishing life.

Moral progress

Moral progress can be real; moral relativism (as in Sartre's radical choice) is unsustainable. The abolition of slavery marked an 'advance in moral sensibility' (Warnock, 1992), as did the 1978 report's abolition of the concept of ineducability. The latter advance has not, however, been fully realised in education.

Love or cherishing

For an advance in moral sensibility, we must accept true conversation, expressive of love, as essential to true teaching. There is a sense, as Kant says, in which love cannot be commanded; but there exists a *kind* of love that can be cultivated or even taught. Kant called it 'practical love'; Aristotle called it *philia* (normally translated as friendship), describing this as a virtue, with emotional and intellectual aspects, that is acquired through learning. *Philia* exists not only between friends in the familiar sense but between parents and children, teachers and pupils. A higher form of love is expressed by the Greek term *agape*.

This corresponds to the Latin *caritas*, related to 'charity' and 'cherishing', and is directed not only towards those we like or to whom we are related but also (often with great effort) towards those we dislike. Teachers sometimes dislike their pupils, and we need a frank exploration of what this means.

Moral progress is not just about the affirmation of moral truths; it is also about advances in feeling or sensibility. The 1978 Warnock Report paves the way for these. What it calls 'knowledge and appreciation' has a deeper layer in concepts like love and cherishing. The philosophical bottom line, essential for special education, is that the tired dichotomy between thought and feeling must be imaginatively overthrown. We must learn to *feel wisely*, not to mention *think lovingly*, and teach teachers to do the same.

References

Cigman, R. (2018) *Cherishing and the good life of learning: Ethics, education, upbringing*. London: Bloomsbury Press.

Dunne, J. (2005) 'What's the good of education?' in W. Carr (ed.) *The RoutledgeFalmer reader in philosophy of education*. London: Routledge.

McKie, R. (2005) *There's something about Mary....* Available online: www.theguardian.com/uk/2005/jun/12/schools.education. Accessed on: 31 August 2018.

Tharp, R.G. and Gallimore, R. (1988) *Rousing minds to life*. Cambridge: Cambridge University Press.

Warnock, M. (1992) 'Education with a moral', in M. Warnock (ed.) *The uses of philosophy*. Oxford: Blackwell.

15 The case for a broader policy framework for special needs and inclusive education

Where we could go next

Brahm Norwich

Where are we now?

In this chapter, I aim to focus on problems in the special educational needs (SEN) and inclusion policy field, which derive from the Warnock legacy, and to suggest a policy perspective that might move us on in a positive direction. These problems can be attributed to the focus on individual needs assessment and legal protections for provision, as implemented since the 1981 Education Act. Though the Warnock Report was broad in its coverage, its legislative translation into the statutory statementing system has dominated the field right up to the latest changes in the Children and Families Act 2014. There has been little change in the basic system despite the refinements by successive governments. Although the latest legislation was promoted as 'a radically different system' (DfE, 2011), the basic design of a protected individual identification and assessment system of additional needs and provision is still the cornerstone of the system.

The SEN system in England is characterised by complexity and dependence on the wider system with negative effects. Figure 15.1 shows a simplified version of the context in which the SEN system operates. At the centre is the SEN system of individual needs assessment and provision protections, which is the responsibility of local authorities. However, alongside this is the parallel and overlapping system of anti-disability discrimination legislation, now under the Equality Act 2010. This introduces the dual systems of definitions and duties.

While local authorities are responsible for Education, Health and Care Plan (formerly Statements) protections, their powers have been weakened by the new governance system of academies and free schools, with greater reliance on market forces in the school system.

Figure 15.1 also shows the interdependence of the National Curriculum and assessment arrangements and Ofsted accountability on

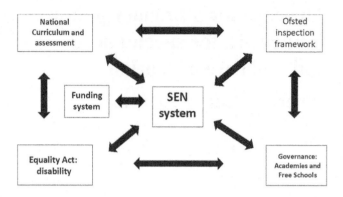

Figure 15.1 Interdependence of the SEN system with other subsystems.

the SEN system. Recent changes to the National Curriculum have resulted in a narrowing of what is learned and how it is assessed. Despite changes to the Ofsted inspection framework, the centrality of the academic progress criteria has been retained (Douglas *et al.*, 2017). Figure 15.1 also represents the impact of reduced funding on, among other things, decreased support staffing in schools and increased pressure for more statutory assessment and Education, Health and Care Plans (EHCPs) (DfE, 2018).

Based on this interdependence analysis, it is clear that the interests of those with SEN and disabilities require a broader position that focusses on the availability of provision and its adaptation and flexibility in inclusive ways. The legal protections currently used for individualised assessment and provision planning could also apply to appropriate general provision. The implication is that there could be a reduced focus on individual assessment and provision planning, and more focus on general provision planning for those with SEN with a presumption for inclusive ways.

This could translate into providing statutory assessment only when parents opt for it, by contrast to the current statutory system for all individual plans. A legacy of the focus on planning for individual needs, which stemmed from the Warnock Enquiry, has been the neglect of protections for the planning focus on general provision. Under the latest SEN Code of Practice (DfE, 2015) the local offer is meant not only to provide information to parents and carers of children with SEN and disabilities on the additional provision available to them but also to provide a process by which, through consultation, provision might be developed. This, for example, is one function of Parent and Carer

Forums. Though the most recent SEN Code of Practice recognises the relationship between individual EHCPs and population needs for provision planning purposes, there is no clear operational system that connects these foci.

Broader policy framework and perspective: where to go next

So, there is a need to adopt a broader policy framework in which SEN and disability in education is interconnected with other aspects of education and is seen in terms of issues about markets and regulation; what is public and private; what is global, national and local; and what is generic and specialised. As the introduction of the EHCP process shows, the framework goes beyond education into other areas of national policy, such as health and social services. How SEN and disability is caught up in wider policy and political processes has to be addressed.

What follows is also informed by a perspective that recognises that policy depends on several basic values, some of which can come into tension during the process of policy formation. And, as various theorists have suggested, these tensions can lead to dilemmas of plural democracy (Dahl, 1982; Berlin, 1990). There are possible tensions between: equality (same) vs. equity (fairness); choice (preference) vs. equity (fairness); participation vs. protection; and how differentiation and difference is positioned as enabling vs. stigmatising. In recognising plural values, it means that when these values cannot be reconciled fully, there may need to be some balancing, some hard choices with some loss of values. To have, for example, choice and equity, some balancing or 'trade-off' is required (Norwich, 2014).

Crouch's (1990) post-democracy perspective is also relevant to this analysis of education policy. In a post-democracy, there are elections with governments falling and there is freedom of speech. But democracy is progressively limited: a small, detached elite taking tough decisions; abuses of democratic institutions; politicians having a poor reputation and lacking trust with the population through the use of spin and hype; and policy development seen in terms of political expedience. As causes of post-democracy, Crouch identified: i) privatisation, the entanglement of public and private sectors, and globalisation; ii) fewer common goals for diverse groups to identify with, more divisiveness and the rise of populist parties; and iii) unbalanced public debates with a poor-quality national discussion.

Expressions of post-democracy can be seen in some of the current failures of education policy formation. New governments tend to deny positive accomplishments by previous governments. Policies are adopted for short-term political gain with rhetorical and real zigzagging rather than for well-founded policy reasons. There has been a breakdown in the relationship between government policy, empirical evidence and professional knowledge, and a tendency to project and justify a false sense of certainty about education policy, with an unwillingness to recognise tensions and uncertainties.

One way forward would be to establish an Education Framework Commission (EFC) to work on the assumption that policy is formed as a settlement that reconciles contrary value positions. The Commission would aim to design a ten-year consensual educational policy framework, within which the current and future governments will work, and that would be renewed after this period. The aim of an EFC would be to:

- raise the level of national educational policy discussion and debate
- design a shared and informed medium-term (e.g. ten-year) education policy framework
- seek and maximise common ground across different social interests, outside the political market of politicians attracting voters at elections
- represent key stakeholders, including representatives from political parties; teachers and school leaders; parent/carers; pupils; local authorities and middle tier organisations; key bodies, such as Ofsted; third-sector and voluntary groups; employers and business; unions and professional associations; etc.
- break down unnecessary polarisations through adopting a position about the role of academic and professional research and evaluation in informing policy and practice
- lobby political parties and MPs to enact legislation to establish the ten-year binding framework for future education legislation, along the lines of climate change legislation.

It is clear that such an EFC would resemble some current practices, such as Parliamentary Select Committees and reviews, such as the Cambridge Primary Review (2009) and the Warnock Enquiry. But it would differ in some key aspects. It would be independent of government, and it would actively seek public deliberation and consensus formation. It would also provide a holistic overview and engage with different groups with differing ideologies. Finally, it would necessarily be funded through the voluntary and charitable sector.

Expectations, risks and implications for special needs and inclusive education

An EFC promises benefits but has risks too. It could be an opportunity to increase national participation in debates about education and so increase understanding, which is itself a public and political educational activity. It would seek to involve people who disagree with each other to listen to and engage with one another. This would be facilitated by activities taking place outside the electoral cycle (e.g. ahead of a general election). Though finding common ground is challenging, there are established strategies that could be deployed, such as values clarification, conflict resolution, citizen shift approaches, futures thinking and citizens' juries.

The aim would also be to formulate the framework in as specific terms as possible to avoid excessive use of constructive ambiguity. It would be expected that the framework would be open to some degree of interpretation by political parties, so enabling ideological differences to emerge at election time. An EFC could reconnect policymakers with citizens by being responsive to parents/carers, children and young people, and professional and citizen interests, and so raise the horizons of the education system.

However, there are risks that an EFC could become marginalised by not managing to engage a wide group of stakeholders with diverse views and values. It might also not engage the political class and be rejected by politicians and political parties. An EFC organisation might also be captured by a group not committed to its principles. Achieving consensus beyond vague generalities might also prove to be very hard to achieve. But the EFC process would still be worthwhile, despite these risks. Even if political parties would not adopt the negotiated framework, it would still be a useful basis for evaluating their education policymaking.

Given the minority status of the special needs and inclusive education field and its interdependences, a focus on change to the wider system is required. I have suggested that to move on from too much emphasis on an individualised focus to one with more balance between a provision and an individualised focus, we need some change in policymaking that deals with our democratic deficit. What is proposed is not some 'third way' approach, as it assumes that ideological differences remain, but an approach that can be moderated by consensus-seeking strategies that test, renew and build on what we have in common. Of course, these approaches can be tried in other key policy areas, such as health, social care and beyond, but education is a good place to start.

If successful then other frameworks for social care and health could link with the education framework. Here is a proposal that could renew ideas and values about the nature of schooling that takes genuine account of SEN and disabilities.

References

Berlin, I. (1990) *The crocked timber of humanity.* London: Fontana Press.

Crouch, C. (2000) *Coping with post-democracy.* London: Fabian Society.

Dahl, R.A. (1982) *Dilemmas in pluralist democracy: Autonomy and control.* Newhaven, CT: Yale University Press.

Department for Education (DfE) (2015) *Special educational needs and disability code of practice: 0 to 25 years.* London: DfE.

Department for Education (DfE) (2018) *Special educational needs in England: January 2018.* London: DfE. Available online: www.gov.uk/government/statistics/special-educational-needs-in-england-january-2018. Accessed on: 6 August 2018.

Department for Education (DfE) (2011) *Support and aspiration: A new approach to special educational needs and disability.* London: DfE.

Douglas, G., Easterlow, G., Ware, J. and Heavey, A. (2017) *A worthwhile investment? Assessing and valuing educational outcomes for children and young people with SEND. SEN Policy Research Forum.* Available online: https://blogs.exeter.ac.uk/sen-policyforum/past-policy-papers/. Accessed on: 31 July 2018.

Norwich, B. (2014) *Addressing tensions and dilemmas in inclusive education. Living with uncertainty.* London: Routledge.

16 Looking forward

Using the Warnock Report to chart a way forward

Rob Webster

In my earlier chapter on the brief history of the Warnock Report, I suggested that we should neither seek to emulate nor replace the Warnock Report but use it to inform the further development of inclusive approaches to educating children and young people with special educational needs and disabilities (SEND). In this final chapter, I will discuss how – against the backdrop of some particular contemporary challenges – the education system in England might successfully educate, and not just accommodate, pupils with SEND. I will draw on the contributions to this book to identify some key areas for development, in terms of schools, culture, teachers and teaching, policy and research.

Supply and demand

Pupil numbers are rising. The most recent official pupil projection data report that the secondary school population in England will increase by as much as 15 per cent over the next seven years (DfE, 2018a). By 2023, secondary mainstream settings will need to have found the space for an additional 376,000 young people and a further 52,000 pupils in the two years after that.

If current statistics on prevalence are any indication (DfE, 2018b), by 2023, we can expect at least 45,300 (10.6 per cent) of these extra secondary-aged pupils to have SEND. A further 6,800 (1.6 per cent) will have needs complex enough to qualify for an Education, Health and Care Plan (EHCP). The geographic distribution of these young people will, of course, be uneven. But if it were even, it would mean each existing secondary mainstream school in England would need to accommodate 15 additional pupils with SEND, two of whom would have an EHCP.[1]

In line with this general trend, the DfE projects that the population of secondary-aged pupils in state-funded special schools in England to also grow. The modelling shows an increase of 15 per cent per cent by 2023; thereafter, numbers plateau (DfE, 2018a). The same data, meanwhile, show that pupil rolls in alternative provision and pupil referral units (hereon, referred to collectively as AP) are set to boom. Taken together, from a 2018 baseline, populations in these settings – 80 per cent of which are identified as having SEND (DfE, 2018c) – will increase by 19 per cent by 2023 and by 25 per cent by 2025. In terms of raw numbers, between 2018 and 2023, the special school population is anticipated to grow by 10,000 pupils, and the AP population will increase by 3,000.

A population rise of this magnitude means more schools and more school places will be needed. This leads inevitably to questions about capacity. If you think the solution to a 15 per cent increase in secondary-aged pupils with SEND is, in part or in whole, to increase the capacity in settings outside mainstream schools, consider this. Special school rolls average around 117 pupils, and AP average around 47 pupils.[2] The expected growth in pupil numbers in these settings is equivalent to the combined rolls of around 150 specialist schools. So, just keeping pace with projected demand requires the government to open 30 new non-mainstream schools per year, for the next five years.

The auguries of this are not good. Since 2012/2013, the DfE has managed to open, at most, just six new special schools a year. The rate at which new APs are coming on stream is actually slowing up. Having opened 24 schools in the three years following the 2012 Taylor Review on improving the quality of AP (Taylor, 2012), the DfE has averaged just four new provisions each year since.

So, given this, now would be a good time to increase mainstream schools' capacity to accommodate pupils with EHCPs (i.e. those who might otherwise attend a special school or AP). However, the opposite seems to be happening. In 2017, 40 per cent of secondary schools had a SEND unit or resourced provision (RP);[3] a year later it fell to 35 per cent. In just 12 months, there has been a 11 per cent reduction in the number of secondary schools with a base for pupils with additional needs (DfE, 2018b). This loss of 151 units and RPs is largely attributable to the diminution in the amount of additional funding that schools receive from local authorities to maintain these bases.

To summarise, then, official data point to a sharp and sustained increase in the population of young people with SEND, but the indications are that the supply of special provisions will not meet demand.

To compound matters, there is also a supply and demand problem relating to teacher retention and recruitment. More pupils mean more teachers, yet exit rates are rising year-on-year across the sector and fastest among special schools (Sibieta, 2018). One in five places for secondary initial teacher training (ITT) are vacant (Hazell, 2018). An analysis by *Tes* (spring 2018) revealed that to stay in line with the average pupil-teacher ratio since 2005 (15.1 pupils to one teacher), the number of secondary teachers will need to increase by 22.5 per cent by 2024: that is 47,000 additional teachers (Hazell, 2018).

Both provision and resources for SEND look set to remain limited and stretched. It is a good bet that, in the coming years, what resources there are (including new schools) will be targeted at meeting the needs of the rising secondary-aged population at the expense of the primary sector. But as even this seems likely to fall short of demand, it increases the need for all mainstream schools to play a more active role in local approaches to educating pupils with SEND.

Starting from here

A number of contributors to this book have pointed to the incompatibility between inclusion and the accountability culture that is endemic to the education system in England. This 'hyper-accountability industry', as psychologist Tim O'Brien (2018) calls it, has incubated and intensified a form of protectionism, practised almost exclusively by mainstream schools. In this context, pupils with SEND are seen as liabilities, posing a threat to coveted league table positions and Ofsted inspection ratings. Such are the stakes – forced academisation, the removal of the governing body and/or members of the school leadership team – it has, in a sense, legitimised a set of practices that are not only antithetical to the aims of inclusion but actively detrimental to it.

For example, the need to optimise school performance indicators has been implicated in the steady rise in exclusions (Ofsted/YouGov, 2018). Children and young people identified as having SEND are six times more likely to be permanently excluded from school, compared with those who do not (DfE, 2018d). And then there is the practice of off-rolling, to which young people with SEND are particularly vulnerable. Ofsted (Ofsted/YouGov, 2018) describe off-rolling as 'where pupils are excluded from schools as a means of improving overall results'. This is no niche enterprise. A 2018 investigation by the *Times* found that the GCSE outcomes of more than 30,000 pupils were missing from results tables, despite these pupils appearing on school registers in the past three years (*Tes*, 2018). A representative survey of 1,000 teachers, meanwhile, on their awareness and perceptions of Ofsted (commissioned by the inspectorate) found that 45 per cent teachers had heard of off-rolling taking place, and 21 per cent had seen it happen (Ofsted/YouGov, 2018). Added to this, there is what the education secretary, Damian Hinds (2018), has called 'pre-emptive exclusion': 'where parents looking at secondary schools are actively or in some way subtly discouraged from applying to a particular school for their child'.

As Tara Flood argues, the existential threat to mainstream education affecting more and more pupils with SEND has been aided and abetted by inaccessible examination processes; if pupils cannot take the tests, let alone perform to a desired standard that meaningfully feeds into a school's SATs or GCSE results, they are at risk of being offloaded or effectively barred from some schools. The Children's Commissioner for England reports that nine out of ten mainstream schools are 'benefiting' from having pupils at risk of underachieving leave: 'their GCSE pass rates are higher than they would be if these children had stayed with them until the end of secondary school' (Children's Commissioner, 2017).

So, where do these pupils go? Data from Ofsted reveal that state-funded AP settings are common destinations for pupils transferred out during Key Stage 4 (Bradbury, 2018). The DfE's statistics, meanwhile, show that pupils with EHCPs are increasingly being 'pushed out' of mainstream schools into special schools (Staufenberg, 2018). A DfE-commissioned review of residential special schools and colleges found that many children and young people in these settings came from mainstream schools where 'they felt so unwelcome' (Lenehan and Geraghty, 2017).[4]

This one-way traffic puts pressure on specialist settings. Between 2004 and 2018, the overall stock of state-funded special schools[5] and AP decreased by 11 per cent, while the combined populations attending these settings rose by 22 per cent (DfE, 2018c). Creating new provisions, however, is problematic. While local authorities hold the legal duty to provide special education for pupils with EHCPs, their ability to build new facilities has been constricted by central government. The Conservative government insists that all new schools in England must be free schools, which sit wholly, or in large part, outside the jurisdiction of local authorities. Free schools were not only promoted as a totem of parental choice, but parents and community groups were actively encouraged (and funded) to set up their own free schools, as well as 'take over' special schools to 'prevent [their] unnecessary closure' (DfE, 2011). Writing in *Tes* in May 2018, Baroness Warnock lauded the pledge made by Michael Gove, as education secretary, to widen school choice. In her earlier writing (Warnock, 1985), however, she was critical of running schools 'on the lines of a consumer-orientated service', even prefiguring a predictable issue concerning parent-led free schools:

> A school is not a club or society to be run by its keener members. It is an educational institution with a life and an ethos of its own, with a history and a future which will far outlive the somewhat ephemeral interest in it of any individual parent.

While the free school model might serve the needs of *some* parents – whose children may or may not have SEND – it is poorly aligned to the reality of planning and providing local special education. (The initial interest in parent-led free schools has now, however, tailed off notably (Garry *et al.*, 2018; Roberts, 2018)). As contracts for running free schools are made centrally with the DfE (bypassing local oversight), one might expect there to be some form of system-wide capacity-mapping exercise to ensure the right schools open in the right locations for the children and young people with particular needs. Yet there is no evidence that this has been happening. At the start of the 2018/2019 academic year, there were 59 new special schools and 16 new APs in the planning pipeline (DfE, 2018e). Around half of the new special schools will be for pupils with autism spectrum conditions (Webster, 2018), and only 12 schools overall are planned for the Midlands and the north of England. Ten of the 16 proposed new APs are in these regions (DfE, 2018e).

It is difficult to avoid the conclusion that the opportunity to link the creation of free schools with the 2014 SEND reforms – thereby creating a coordinated national strategy for SEND – was completely missed. It is, of course, not a laughing matter, but to paraphrase the hackneyed old joke about the tourist in Ireland asking a local for directions to Dublin, if you were building an inclusive education system in England, you would not start from here. Here, however, is where we are. So, what can be done?

Schools

To begin, there is a fundamental issue with hardware: the shortage of schools and school places, which is particularly acute in the face of a rising secondary-aged population. Part of the solution to meeting additional needs could be to increase the number of small specialist units, collocated with, or housed within, mainstream schools. While the official statistics show that SEN units and RP are on the critical list, expanding this capacity and/or amalgamating bases into larger generic needs units is a more efficient use of scant resources, compared with new school builds.

Such bases provide opportunities for pupils with SEND to be taught in mainstream lessons alongside their peers. Suggesting this might be a model for the future, Mary Warnock (2007) identified the potential for staff working in these units and staff working in the main school to 'cooperate socially'. She went on to say, rightly, that 'decisions [to expand such units] must be taken on the basis of evidence'. But the research on the overall effectiveness of collocated facilities is thin. An urgent review could, therefore, provide the evidence on which proposals for expansion could be based. More broadly, it is worth repeating Warnock's call for 'well-funded and well-publicised research... on how children with different disabilities flourish or fail to flourish in different settings' (Warnock, 2007) as a basis for informing future plans for the overall system architecture of schools.

More immediately, there is a policy impediment to expanding the capacity of existing schools, which must be removed. Seventy per cent of secondary schools in England are academies, and as it stands, local authorities have no power to compel academies to create more spaces for pupils. As long as local authorities provide the bulk of the funding for SEN units and RPs, academies are likely to continue to support them. However, cuts to local council budgets pose a threat not just to further expansion but to their very future. Local authorities should either be given the power to compel academies to expand, or the restrictions on building new schools should be lifted. Arguably, both actions are required.

Culture change

Second, there is the relationship between attitudes and practices, and how the former underpin and inform the extent to which inclusive approaches are adopted and actualised throughout the sector. The perverse incentives that give rise to controversial practices hostile to learners with SEND, such as off-rolling, suggest that 50 years on from the start of the campaigns that resulted in children and young people with disabilities safeguarding their right to an education, we are, as Maggie Atkinson and Tara Flood explain, still some distance from securing their right to a *quality* education. Head teacher, Vic Goddard, forcefully concludes that funding is 'a killer for inclusion'. But as he, Nancy Gedge and Sally Phillips make clear, attitudes towards including children and young people with SEND, and their families, are at least as important as funding. As the public sector spending cuts of the early 1980s bit, Mary Warnock (1985) wrote: 'we are beginning to learn that money alone is not a remedy for educational inadequacy'. Indeed, as we shall come to, education quality is, as Warnock went on the say, 'more a matter of human relations than finance'.

The systemic change that the contributions to this book are calling for will be more authentic and sustainable if it comes from the teaching profession, than if it arrives via top-down edict. Off-rolling is a good example of how the latter prompts schools to develop survival techniques. Though clearly needed, action against off-rolling – such as a financial penalty or withholding a favourable Ofsted rating – will not improve the classroom experience for pupils with SEND. We will return to teacher and school leader agency shortly, but we must consider here the role of policymakers and regulators.

In an appearance at an Education Committee hearing in July 2018, Baroness Warnock observed that Ofsted's focus on 'academic excellence' meant that it had a 'contradictory role' with respect to inclusion (HC 968). The inspectorate, she suggested, 'ought to be giving acknowledgement to those schools which are genuinely inclusive, and take real pride in what they do for children with special needs'. Accountability processes, then, need to incentivise better behaviour.

One option would be to make SEND a limiting judgement for inspection: a school's overall grade would not be allowed to exceed its grade relating to SEND provision and outcomes. Another suggestion, put forward by the Education Committee in its report, *Forgotten children: Alternative provision and the scandal of ever increasing exclusions*, is for the government and Ofsted to 'introduce an inclusion measure or criteria that sits within schools to incentivise schools to be more inclusive' (House of Commons Education Committee, 2018). Notwithstanding the effect a trigger word like 'measure' can have within the teaching profession, and the tendency for any measure in education to succumb to Goodhart's Law (when a measure becomes a target, it ceases to be a good measure), this is an interesting, though underdeveloped, idea. Any meaningful school-level indicator of inclusion requires a supra-dimension to determine how inclusive a school is relative to its neighbours. In other words, does it admit its fair share of children and young people with SEND within the local community, or does it, to use Damian Hinds phrase, manage its admissions using pre-emptive exclusion?

If agency is the better lever, and if, as Vic Goddard says, inclusion is about 'botheredness', how might we encourage and reward positive efforts among school leaders and teachers? Perhaps we could incentivise individuals by hardwiring excellence for SEND into performance management and promotion systems, developing career progression for teachers and leaders that is contingent on evidencing practice that improves experiences and outcomes for pupils with SEND.

On a more immediate term and routine basis, another way we might modify behaviour is by changing our language. As several contributors to this book, including Mary Warnock, have indicated, how we talk about SEND has a considerable bearing on attitudes, approaches and expectations. Jon Severs writes with acuity and honesty about how portrayals of SEND in the media perpetuate narratives that are centred more on placating the uncomfortable feelings people without disability have about those with SEND and how the SEND community deserves a greater, more authentic voice. There has been undoubted progress, but we need to keep pushing against the pernicious effects of labelling. Inclusion is implicitly about valuing youngsters; so, 40 years from now, labels such as 'low ability' and 'bottom set' should have become as redundant as 'backward' and 'retarded'. Paul Warren concludes that developing children and young people's 'resilience and grit and cultivating a growth mindset are as important as any reasonable adjustment'. The language associated with these approaches is necessarily positive, founded on having high expectations of learners, and is an intrinsic component of an inclusive pedagogy.

Teachers and teacher training

Third, we need to acknowledge where our preoccupations with school organisation are holding us back. Research shows that pupils with SEND tend to be taught together in small 'low ability' classes containing additional adults. The evidence is also clear that setting and streaming, and an over-reliance on teaching assistants (TAs) to teach pupils with SEND, are associated with lower-quality teaching and learning experiences, and poorer outcomes for pupils in these classes (Taylor *et al.*, 2016; Webster *et al.*, 2010).

The over-reliance on TAs to teach pupils with SEND has become particularly problematic (Webster, 2015) and is an indication that the structural model of inclusion we have drifted towards over recent decades reflects a failure to fully address long-standing questions about how pupils with SEND are taught in mainstream settings. There is much that schools can do to improve how they deploy TAs and offer the flexible approaches to grouping and lessons (Webster *et al.*, 2016), but the effects will be limited without significant improvements to teaching.

As the Warnock Enquiry concluded, increasing teachers' knowledge of SEND was, and remains, of 'utmost importance'. Now, as in 1978, 'it is imperative that every teacher should appreciate that up to one child in five is likely to require some form of special educational help at some time during his school career' (Section 12.1). While SEND now has a higher profile in ITT than it did 40 years ago, as Alan Hodkinson highlights, it remains something of a Cinderella subject.

In the 1970s, data on newly qualified teachers' (NQTs) levels of preparation and skill for teaching pupils with SEND was extremely limited. The Warnock Report cites results from a 1977 survey of NQTs in Scotland, which found that 58 per cent of new teachers felt 'inadequately' prepared for teaching pupils with SEND. The most recent survey of NQTs in England (2017) found that, of all aspects of their preparation for teaching, SEND was one of the two areas[6] in which they felt least prepared: 53 per cent reported that their ITT 'prepared them well' for teaching pupils with SEND, and 40 per cent said it 'prepared them well' to assess the progress of pupils with SEND.[7]

Most recently, Baroness Warnock referred to coverage of SEND as a 'great deficiency' in teacher training: 'a kind of extra... not really central to teacher training' (HC 968, 2018). The Warnock Committee's recommendation of a 'special education element' into ITT, therefore, remains pertinent. So too is the Warnock Committee's observation that SEND coverage should be efficiently and carefully woven through the ITT curriculum – not tacked on as stand-alone content, which may be vulnerable to the chop in an overloaded timetable.

If teachers are the agents of change, then it follows that an important area for action in bringing about a more inclusive system is the improvement of teachers' confidence and competence regarding teaching for SEND. And not just as part of ITT but habitually, via opportunities for ongoing professional development and reflection. If creative curriculum design, inclusive pedagogy and more purposeful approaches to how schools and classrooms are organised for learners with SEND are to materialise, it is essential that teachers develop and maintain a strong base of knowledge and skills.

Andria Zafriakou's contribution to this book gives us insight into how this can work in practice and the impact it can have on a young person with complex needs. Her relentless curiosity about the lives and backgrounds of the disadvantaged learners she teaches and her thoughtful acts (Aitkenhead, 2018) are the basis for enduring 'authentic relationships'. It is these bonds of trust – vital for the most vulnerable pupils who perhaps have limited experience of nurturing relationships with adults – that allow them to thrive in school.

The interview with Mary Warnock in Chapter 2 covers very similar terrain. For her, the importance of teachers' attitudes to their children (irrespective of need), and the ways in which they engage *with* their pupils – what she calls the 'personal connections' – are the foundation on which educational success is built. Baroness Warnock identifies 'cherish', 'nurture' and 'love' and the underlying human and humane qualities necessary for establishing authentic relationships. Ruth Cigman extends this theme in her chapter, arguing that 'advances in feeling or sensibility' are necessary for moral progress.

Mary Warnock suggests that ITT 'doesn't give enough attention to the personal relationship that must hold between teachers and pupils' in order for them to flourish. She argues that understanding how to make personal connections with pupils is in short supply within the profession, and that this (as well as SEND) ought to be 'the core of teacher training'. The role of the teacher, as Mary Warnock sees it, 'isn't a matter of conveying information to their pupils, but a matter of loving them'. Implicit in Andria Zafirakou's account of teaching Joe, it is not either but both: an engaging curriculum taught in a benign environment, drained of the low-level toxic influence of accountability, provides a safe space within which trust is forged and pupils can flourish.

The extent to which the skills required to make personal connections with pupils – let alone 'love' them – are *teachable* is, perhaps, an open question. Furthermore, even if it were possible to shoehorn relevant coverage into the crowded ITT curriculum, it seems incompatible with what Alan Hodkinson describes as the 'technicist approach of auditable competencies' that passes for qualified teacher status assessment. As it stands, relationship building is also incompatible with both the philosophy of teaching promoted by the current Conservative government, which has little time for so-called 'child-centred' approaches, and the reality of working within the 'hyper-accountability industry'.

Hostility to 'child-centred' approaches is not good news for an education system that is, so to speak, having inclusion forced on it due to failures in planning and underfunding. If teaching is not child-centred – especially for those whose learning needs are greater and potentially more complex than most of their peers – then what is it? If it cannot *be* child-centred, due to pressures of teacher workload, accountability and staffing shortages, then these issues must not be ignored and must be addressed; because as long as this remains the case, all the indications are that vulnerable learners will remain at high risk of marginalisation.

The policy case for inclusion

There are good reasons policymakers should consider supporting system reform that would lead to more inclusive forms of schooling. There is a maturing evidence base that suggests inclusive educational settings can confer short-term and long-term benefits for *all* learners, in terms of improvements in reading and mathematics, higher rates of attendance, increased likelihood of completing formal education and participation in post-secondary education. A greater proportion of pupils taught in inclusive environments go on to find employment and live independently, compared to those who are not (Kalambouka *et al.*, 2005; Hehir *et al.*, 2016). Young people with disabilities who attend segregated settings, on the other hand, are less likely to have friendships and social networks in their adult life (European Agency for Special Needs and Inclusive Education, 2018). A 2017 meta-analysis by Szumski *et al.* which covered a sample of almost 4,800,000 pupils, found a positive and statistically significant, though weak, effect of the presence of pupils with SEND in mainstream classrooms on the learning of pupils without SEND. In other words, including pupils with learning difficulties in mainstream lessons has no detrimental effect on other pupils. This, in effect, kicks the legs out from one of the most persistent arguments against inclusion.

Contributors to this book have rightly emphasised the social justice and moral case for inclusion. Peter Imray argues that there 'really is no point to educational inclusion if it merely reinforces social exclusion'. Compelling though the moral case is, we should perhaps lose our shyness about advancing the economic case for inclusion, too. There are significant long-term economic and social costs involved in failing children and young people with SEND, as revealed in the correlations between SEND and exclusion; low attainment; being neither in education, employment or training; and youth crime (House of Commons Education and Skills Committee, 2006). Early, sustained intervention not only saves money and lives but also enriches society and the national economy. A review of the literature for the European Commission (European Agency for Special Needs and Inclusive Education, 2018) found evidence to suggest that young people with disabilities who attend an inclusive setting are more likely to gain employment and be financially independent on leaving education. Such data should be persuasive to any national government or administration that lays claim to evidence-based policymaking. This brings us, finally, to the role of research.

Research in SEND

The Warnock Report set out a range of areas in which the committee felt research was urgently needed (Section 18.15). As Klaus Wedell reminds us, Warnock's recommendation that a government-funded Special Education Research Group (SERG) should be established to 'provide a synoptic view of what is going on and offer guidance on priorities' (Section 18.11) was not pursued. Nonetheless, several areas of research on the committee's priority list[8] were addressed in the seminal One in Five study, which investigated special needs in primary schools (Croll and Moses, 1985).

SEND research, and educational research in general, has thrived in the UK and internationally in the past four decades. Yet the SEND population is insufficiently represented in large-scale longitudinal data collection efforts (such as the UK Millennium Cohort Study) that have become indispensable in helping to address a wealth of research and policy questions. Any list of SEND research priorities for the next 40 years should have a large-scale longitudinal cohort study of children with SEND near the top.

What might be our other research imperatives, and how might we go about operationalising them? As noted, there is compelling evidence to support a policy agenda to make the education of pupils with SEND more inclusive. This may be desirable, but is it doable? While researchers appear able to define features and impacts of inclusive settings, the characteristics of teaching and curricula (the 'how' and the 'what') are less clear. Indeed, the evidence from systematic reviews of the impact of inclusive approaches (e.g. Kalambouka *et al.*, 2005; Hehir *et al.*, 2016) is reticent on the practical issues of implementation. Broad statements about success are worthy but lack precision: it is not exclusively a matter of additional financial resources; more or better training; and teachers and other professionals needing to 'regularly engage in collaborative problem-solving' (Herir *et al.*, 2016). Consequently, the active ingredients of effective 'inclusive' classroom teaching and learning for pupils with (and without) SEND remain elusive. Identifying and validating these characteristics ought to be a priority for future research.

Another focus area is the paucity of quality research evidence, especially in the UK, on pedagogic practice for pupils with SEND in mainstream settings. A systematic literature review by Rix *et al.* (2009) on this topic (for the UK government) yielded 28 papers for in-depth analysis – just 1 per cent of the total they started out with (2,982) – and only ten of these scored well in terms of research design. How, then, do we reconcile this apparent lack of evidence within the literature on what good inclusive practice looks like with the more substantive evidence on impact? One explanation could be that approaches to teaching pupils with learning difficulties are inherently contestable; so-called 'SEND pedagogy/pedagogies' may not be as materially different and distinguishable from approaches that work for all learners as we perhaps intuitively believe (Davis and Florian, 2004). Another explanation might be that teachers are not adept at accurately reporting and describing what they do (Good and Brophy, 2002; Nuthall, 2007), and this may apply equally to SEND (Webster and Blatchford, 2018).

In a careful dissection of the conceptual and practical challenges of defining and operationalising inclusive pedagogy, Norwich (2013) concludes that this term is multilevelled and multidirectional, and used interchangeably to refer to matters relating to what it is (curricula), how it is achieved (approaches to teaching and learning) and where (in which settings) it occurs. In view of this, the contributions of front-line practitioners like Vijita Patel and Andria Zafirakou are central to our collective effort of realising Mary Warnock's educational philosophy. Fuelled by what Ruth Cigman calls thinking that is 'not dry but imaginative, not detached but practically and emotionally engaged', they describe the need for and impact of creative and thoughtful curriculum design and inclusive pedagogy. Paul Warren provides a real-world example of how his junior school provided a 'state-of-the-art electronic typewriter' to assist his writing, and Klaus Wedell points to the potential for digital technology to provide even greater flexibility 'in relation to time and place for learning'.

From her 1978 report onward, Mary Warnock has consistently called for collaboration between researchers, teachers and other professionals in understanding and addressing educational issues, and in advancing and disseminating knowledge and practice: 'The part which teachers can play in research and development is often undervalued and far more encouragement and support needs to be given to them to carry out systematic research' (Section 18.7). The research endeavour for SEND moving forward, therefore, needs to find space for more teacher-researcher partnerships, through which new insights and practices can be developed, tested and mobilised.

Indeed, the kinds of vehicles for achieving this, which the Warnock Committee prefigured in its recommendations relating to evidence-informed practice and practitioner research, have emerged in recent years – although, they are generalist, rather than SEND-specific. Research Schools, for example, mirror the committee's call for local centres 'where research, development and in-service training in special education are based' (Section 18.17). Warnock also envisaged a Special Education Staff College to lead research-informed professional development for teachers via multidisciplinary courses and conferences (Section 18.18). This echoes the aims of the Chartered College of Teaching, which was established in 2017 to support teachers and leaders who want to work in a more effective, informed way.

A SERG for the 2020s could coordinate and perform a range of important functions to raise the profile of SEND and help advance the inclusive education agenda. It would link in to, and bridge between, national and local organisations and networks, both general and SEND-specific. It would also be part of the holistic Education Framework Commission (EFC), outlined by Brahm Norwich in the previous chapter.

Concluding remarks

In conclusion, we must emphasise that organisational changes and additional resources will not be sufficient in themselves to achieve our aims. They must be accompanied by changes in attitudes. Special education must be seen as a form of educational activity no less important, no less demanding and no less rewarding than any other, and teachers, administrators and other professionals engaged in it must have the same commitment to children with special needs as they have to all other children. Nor will it be enough if these changes in attitudes are confined to people engaged in special education. Changes in attitude are also necessary on the part of the public at large. There must be a general acceptance of the idea that special education involves as much skill and professional expertise as any other form of education, and that, in human terms, the returns on resources invested in it are just as great.

(Section 19.35)

It was 'with these thoughts in mind' that *The Report of the Committee of Enquiry into the Education of Handicapped Children and Young People* was submitted to the secretaries of state of England, Scotland

and Wales, in March 1978. More than 40 years on, the Warnock Report endures, a marker of change in the discourse of SEND, with practical proposals still awaiting implementation.

Notes

1 The primary school population is expected to drop by 1 per cent by 2023 and by 2 per cent by 2026.
2 Total state-funded special school population (115,300) and state-funded AP population (16,700) divided by number of state-funded special schools (984) and state-funded AP (352).
3 'Resourced provisions are where places are reserved at a mainstream school for pupils with a specific type of SEN, taught mainly within mainstream classes, but requiring a base and some specialist facilities around the school. SEN units are special provisions within a mainstream school where the children are taught mainly within separate classes' (DfE, 2018f).
4 It is worth noting that there are tens of thousands of additional children – many of whom are highly vulnerable – who are educated outside mainstream or special schools. The Children's Commissioner in England (2017) reports that 'many are effectively "hidden" away in settings where little is known about how well their needs are being met'. There are an estimated 50,000-plus children and young people who are not in education at all; over 6,000 of them may be untraceable.
5 This does not include non-maintained special schools (NMSS). The number of NMSS has decreased by 16 per cent, and the pupil population in these settings has decreased by 25 per cent, over this period (2004–2018).
6 The other area was teaching pupils with English as an additional language: 39 per cent of NQTs felt well prepared to do this.
7 These scores were the average across all NQTs, but there were variations between training routes. NQTs who trained via School Direct reported the greatest levels of satisfaction, while those who trained via the Teach First route reported the lowest. The survey sample was 1,639 NQTs.
8 Specifically: 'forms of school organisation for maladjusted children in ordinary schools and elsewhere'; and 'the slow learner in the ordinary school: effective forms of organisation, curriculum and methods for children with mild or moderate learning difficulties' (Section 18.15).

References

Aitkenhead, D. (2018) 'Best teacher in the world Andria Zafirakou: 'Build trust with your kids – then everything else can happen'', *The Guardian*. Available online: www.theguardian.com/education/2018/mar/23/best-teacher-in-the-world-andria-zafirakou-build-trust-with-your-kids-then-everything-else-can-happen. Accessed on: 24 September 2018.
Bradbury, J. (2018) 'Off-rolling: using data to see a fuller picture', *Ofsted blog*. Available online: https://educationinspection.blog.gov.uk/2018/06/26/

off-rolling-using-data-to-see-a-fuller-picture/. Accessed on: 24 September 2018.

Children's Commissioner (2017) *Briefing. Falling through the gaps in education.* Available online: www.childrenscommissioner.gov.uk/wp-content/uploads/2017/11/BRIEFING-Falling-through-the-gaps-in-education-CCO.pdf. Accessed on: 24 September 2018.

Croll, P. and Moses, D. (1985) *One in five: The assessment and incidence of special education needs.* London: Routledge and Kegan Paul.

Davis, P. and Florian, L. (2004) *Teaching strategies and approaches for pupils with special educational needs: A scoping study. Research Report 516,* London: Dept. for Education and Skills.

Department for Education (2018a) *National pupil projections: July 2018.* Available online: www.gov.uk/government/statistics/national-pupil-projections-july-2018. Accessed on: 24 September 2018.

Department for Education (2018b) *Special educational needs in England: January 2018.* Available online: www.gov.uk/government/statistics/special-educational-needs-in-england-january-2018. Accessed on: 24 September 2018.

Department for Education (2018c) *Schools, pupils and their characteristics: January 2018.* Available online: www.gov.uk/government/statistics/schools-pupils-and-their-characteristics-january-2018. Accessed on: 24 September 2018.

Department for Education (2018d) *Permanent and fixed-period exclusions in England: 2016 to 2017.* Available online: www.gov.uk/government/statistics/permanent-and-fixed-period-exclusions-in-england-2016-to-2017. Accessed on: 24 September 2018.

Department for Education (2018e) *Free schools: Successful applications.* Available online: www.gov.uk/government/publications/free-schools-open-schools-and-successful-applications. Accessed on: 22 August 2018.

Department for Education (2018f) *Special educational needs in England: January 2018. Technical document.* Available online: www.gov.uk/government/statistics/special-educational-needs-in-england-january-2018. Accessed on: 22 August 2018.

Department for Education (2011) *Support and aspiration: A new approach to special educational needs and disability. A consultation.* Available online: www.gov.uk/government/publications/support-and-aspiration-a-new-approach-to-special-educational-needs-and-disability-consultation. Accessed on: 27 November 2018.

European Agency for Special Needs and Inclusive Education (2018) *Evidence of the link between inclusive education and social inclusion: A review of the literature.* Odense: Denmark. Available online: www.european-agency.org/resources/publications/evidence-literature-review. Accessed: 24 September 2018.

Garry, J., Rush, C., Hillary, J., Cullinane, C. and Montacute, R. (2018) *Free for all? Analysing free schools in England, 2018.* Available online: www.nfer.ac.uk/free-for-all-analysing-free-schools-in-england-2018/. Accessed on: 27 November 2018.

Good, T.L. and Brophy, J.E. (2002) *Looking in classrooms*. New York: Harper and Row.

Hazell, W. (2018) 'England needs 47,000 extra secondary teachers', *Tes*. Available online: www.tes.com/news/exclusive-england-needs-47000-extra-secondary-teachers. Accessed on: 24 September 2018.

HC 968 (2018) *Education Committee. Oral evidence: Special educational needs and disabilities*. Available online: http://data.parliament.uk/writtenevidence/committeeevidence.svc/evidencedocument/education-committee/special-educational-needs-and-disabilities/oral/86526.pdf. Accessed on: 17 August 2018.

Hehir, T., Grindal, T., Freeman, B., Lamoreau, R., Borquaye, Y. and Burke, S. (2016) *A summary of the evidence on inclusive education*. Sao Paulo: Instituto Alana. Available online: https://alana.org.br/wp-content/uploads/2016/12/A_Summary_of_the_evidence_on_inclusive_education.pdf. Accessed on: 14 September 2018.

Hinds, D. (2018) *Speech to children's services sector*. Available online: www.gov.uk/government/speeches/education-secretary-makes-inaugural-speech-to-childrens-services-sector. Accessed on: 24 September 2018.

House of Commons Education Committee (2018) *Forgotten children: Alternative provision and the scandal of ever increasing exclusions. Fifth report of session 2017–19*. London: House of Commons. Available online: https://publications.parliament.uk/pa/cm201719/cmselect/cmeduc/342/342.pdf. Accessed on: 6 August 2018.

House of Commons Education and Skills Committee (2006) *Special educational needs. Third report of session 2005–06*. Available online: www.publications.parliament.uk/pa/cm200506/cmselect/cmeduski/478/478i.pdf. Accessed: 27 September 2018.

Kalambouka, A., Farrell, P., Dyson, A. and Kaplan, I. (2005) 'The impact of population inclusivity in schools on student outcomes', *Research Evidence in Education Library*. London: EPPI-Centre, Social Science Research Unit, Institute of Education, University of London. Available online: http://eppi.ioe.ac.uk/cms/Portals/0/PDF per cent20reviews per cent20and per cent-20summaries/incl_rv3.pdf?ver=2006-03-02-124937-203. Accessed on: 23 September 2018.

Lenehan, C. and Geraghty, M. (2017) *Good intentions, good enough? A review of the experiences and outcomes of children and young people in residential special schools and colleges*. Available online: https://councilfordisabledchildren.org.uk/sites/default/files/field/attachemnt/Good_intentions_good_enough_-_a_review_of_residential_special_schools_and_colleges.pdf. Accessed on: 24 September 2018.

Norwich, B. (2013) *Addressing tensions and dilemmas in inclusive education*. Oxon: Routledge.

Nuthall, G. (2007) *The hidden lives of learners*. Wellington: NZCER Press.

O'Brien, T. (2018) 'Diagnosing a crisis of agency', *Tes*. Available online: www.tes.com/news/tes-magazine/tes-magazine/diagnosing-a-crisis-agency. Accessed on: 19 October 2018.

Ofsted/YouGov (2018) Teachers' awareness and perceptions of Ofsted. Teacher Attitude Survey 2018 report. Available online: https://assets.publishing.service. gov.uk/government/uploads/system/uploads/attachment_data/file/734327/ Teachers_Attitude_Survey_2018_awareness_and_perceptions_of_Ofsted_ Final_Report_August_2018.pdf. Accessed on: 24 September 2018.

Rix, J., Hall, K., Nind, M., Sheehy, K. and Wearmouth, J. (2009) 'What pedagogical approaches can effectively include children with special educational needs in mainstream classrooms? A systematic literature review', *Support for Learning*, 24(2), pp. 86–94.

Roberts, J. (2018) 'Whatever happened to parent-led free schools?' *Tes*. Available online: www.tes.com/news/tes-magazine/tes-magazine/whatever-happened-parent-led-free-schools. Accessed on: 27 November 2018.

Sibieta, L. (2018) *The teacher labour market in England. Shortages, subject expertise and incentives*. London: Education Policy Institute. Available online: https://epi.org.uk/publications-and-research/the-teacher-labour-market-in-england/. Accessed on: 24 September 2018.

Staufenberg, J. (2018) 'SEND pupils 'pushed out' of mainstream schools, new data shows', *Schools week*. Available online: https://schoolsweek.co.uk/send-pupils-pushed-out-of-mainstream-schools-new-data-shows. Accessed on: 24 September 2018.

Szumski, G., Smogorzewska, J. and Karwowski, M. (2017) 'Academic achievement of students without special educational needs in inclusive classrooms: A meta-analysis', *Educational Research Review*, 21, pp. 33–54.

Taylor, B., Francis, B., Archer, L., Hodgen, J., Pepper, D., Tereshchenko, A. and Travers, M-C. (2016) 'Factors deterring schools from mixed attainment teaching practice'. *Pedagogy, Culture and Society*, 25(3), pp. 327–345.

Taylor, C. (2012) *Improving alternative provision*. London: Department for Education. Available online: www.gov.uk/government/publications/ improving-alternative-provision. Accessed on: 24 September 2018.

Tes (2018) 'Schools 'off-roll thousands to boost results''. *Tes*. Available online: www.tes.com/news/schools-roll-thousands-boost-results. Accessed on: 24 September 2018.

Warnock, M. (2018) 'Do we need to address a bias towards inclusion?' *Tes*. Available online: www.tes.com/news/do-we-need-address-bias-towards-inclusion. Accessed on: 24 September 2018.

Warnock, M. (2007) 'Foreword', in. R. Cigman (ed.) *Included or excluded? The challenge of the mainstream for some SEN children*. Oxon: Routledge.

Warnock, M. (1985) *Teacher, teach thyself. A new professionalism for our schools*. The Richard Dimbleby Lecture. London: BBC, pp. x–xiv.

Webster, R. (2018) 'Our route to 2026 is a challenge, not a crisis, but we need to act now', *Tes*. Available online: www.tes.com/news/tes-magazine/ tes-magazine/our-route-2026-a-challenge-not-a-crisis-we-need-act-now. Accessed on: 24 September 2018.

Webster, R. (2015) 'The classroom experiences of pupils with special educational needs in mainstream primary schools – 1976 to 2012. What do data from systematic observation studies reveal about pupils' educational experiences over time?' *British Educational Research Journal*, 41(6), pp. 992–1009.

Webster, R. and Blatchford, P. (2018) 'Making sense of "teaching", "support" and "differentiation": The educational experiences of pupils with Education, Health and Care Plans and Statements in mainstream secondary schools', *European Journal of Special Needs Education*, DOI: 10.1080/08856257.2018.1458474

Webster, R., Blatchford, P., Bassett, P., Brown, P., Martin, C. and Russell, A. (2010) 'Double standards and first principles: Framing teaching assistant support for pupils with special educational needs', *European Journal of Special Needs Education*, 25(4), pp. 319–336.

Index

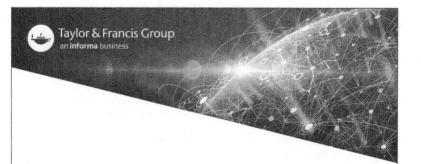